HAINTS, HAUNTS & HISTORY'S MYSTERIES

Of Southeast Missouri
Vol. I

Esther M. Ziock-Carroll

DEDICATION

To our dog, Sandy, who came back to visit us
twice after she died.

CONTENTS

ACKNOWLEDGEMENTS

Thank you to Steven LaChance for suggesting I write a book about my historical research, paranormal & cemetery adventures.

Thank you to my friend Rodney Wilson for helping me proof-read my manuscripts.

And a special thank you to my husband of 47+ years, Gene Carroll, for his support and encouragement of all my research and writing projects.

INTRODUCTION

Southeast Missouri is located in the ancient St. Francois and Ozark Mountains. The St. Francois Mountains were formed by volcanic activity 1.5 billion years ago and are composed of the oldest rocks in the state. The Ozark Mountains, which form a plateau around the St. Francois Mountains, were formed millions of years ago by ancient seas and prehistoric upheavals.

The first people to inhabit southeast Missouri were the pre-historic Indians. The Kimmswick Bone Bed in Jefferson County is one of the most extensive ice age fossil deposits in the country. Two Clovis era spear points that were found next to mastodon bones proves that humans coexisted with prehistoric animals 14,000 years ago.

Southeast Missouri is bordered on the east by the great Mississippi River. In 1673 Father Jacques Marquette and Louis Joliet, while making a voyage on this river, were the first Europeans to set foot in what would later become the State of Missouri.

The first white settlers in southeast Missouri were the French Canadians who came across the Mississippi River from Illinois in the early 1700s and began mining lead, an abundant mineral in this area at that time.

El Camino Real, established in the 1700s, was a trail through southeast Missouri leading from New Madrid to St. Louis. It was used by the Spanish, French and Indians. It is considered the oldest road in Missouri. Part of this trail is now called Telegraph Road in south St. Louis.

In the 1700s Americans began arriving from the eastern states, acquired land grants and built more villages and towns. Subsequently southeast Missouri is home to some of the oldest history, homes and hauntings in the state.

I've been a genealogist/historian since 1971 and have done extensive research on the history of Washington County. I began getting into ghost hunting in 2005 and was a member of several paranormal groups. I have participated in some of the investigations mentioned in this book. In 2011 my husband, Gene, and I designated ourselves as the "Ozark Haint Hunters".

The Lucas - Wilcox house was one of my first investigations. It is believed to have been built in the mid 1800s and has a limestone foundation and log floor joists. It is on lot #17 in Caledonia's historic district and is listed on the National Register of Historic Places.

This building is located across the street from the haunted Caledonia Wine Cottage. While some of the investigators were busy in the Wine Cottage about a half dozen of us went to the Lucas-Wilcox house. Someone had a ghost detector that had a light on it that was supposed to change color when a ghost was in the room. In one of the back rooms of the house the ghost detector was placed in the middle of the floor and we all formed a large circle around it and then the lights were turned off. And we silently waited...........and waited...........we all just stood there............... quietly watching that light.

After a few minutes I'm thinking to myself, "OMG!! Here I am standing in a dark room in an old vacant house with people I don't know, staring at a tiny light in the middle of the floor waiting for a ghost to show up. Am I crazy or what?!"

Well the light never did anything but when we did the same thing in a front room of the house I felt a slight, gentle, cool breeze softly touch the right side of my face even though the ghost detector never changed color. I had always thought that if anything supernatural ever happened to me I would run away screaming in terror. But that soft breeze seemed to settle my nerves and I continue to do ghost hunting whenever I am able. But I still wear my running shoes – just in case.

WASHINGTON COUNTY

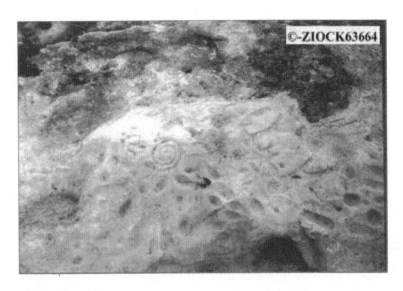

RELIGIOUS CULT: The Indians of the Mississippian period participated in a religious cult that made spiritual/occult carvings of thunderbirds, mace, sunbursts, fertility, snakes, quadrangles and other symbols called "petroglyphs" in outcroppings of dolomite rock on a mountain above Big River. It is believed that this area was a sacred spot and that the symbols had magical and religious qualities. This site is located in Washington State Park in the northeast edge of Washington County. It contains the largest group of petroglyphs yet discovered in Missouri and is listed on the National Register of Historic Places.

BEZIDEK HILL: I read somewhere once that Bezidek Hill is supposedly haunted by the ghost of an old Indian chief. The Hill, which has an elevation of approximately 850 feet, used to be a lead mine. It is located in northeast Washington County near Shibboleth.

AN OLD LEGEND: Francois Azor, a.k.a. "The Breton", was a retired soldier from Ft. DeChartres, Illinois. According to an old legend Azor and his guide, Peter Boyer, circa 1774, were tracking a bear in what would later become Washington County. Azor built a campfire next to what was thought to be a tree root. When the tree root melted Azor realized it was lead.

Another version of the legend and the most widely accepted version is that Francois Azor and his guide, Peter Boyer, were tracking a bear along a creek in what would later become Washington County, Missouri, when Azor stumbled over an outcropping of lead.

HISTORY OF MINE AU BRETON / POTOSI:

Azor, "the Breton" eventually received a grant for four arpents of land on the south side of Breton Creek. Crude stone furnaces were built and a primitive mining village quickly sprang up. Mine Au Breton became the most intensely worked lead mine with black slave labor being used at some of the mines.

In the 1790s Moses Austin arrived and he received a grant for 7,153 arpents of land and transformed lead mining and smelting into Missouri's first major industry. He sank the first mine shaft in Missouri and built the first reverberatory furnace west of the Mississippi River. As a condition of Austin's grant Austin provided many improvements for this area. He and his 40 to 50 slaves and employees built bridges, roads, a store, a blacksmith shop, a flour mill, a saw mill, a shot tower, and turned out the first sheet lead and cannonballs made in Missouri. In 1807 the village of Mine Au Breton had about 40 houses. From the time of the discovery of lead a continuous settlement has existed here.

Washington County was organized in August 1813. The influential Moses Austin donated 40 acres of land on the north side of Breton Creek for establishment of a county seat. The town was named Potosi. For all of his improvements of the area and his donation of the land for the county seat Moses Austin is credited with being the founding father of

Potosi. Mine Au Breton on the south side of Breton Creek and Potosi on the north side eventually consolidated under the sole name of Potosi.

DEATH OF MOSES AUSTIN: Moses Austin is not only credited with being the founding father of Potosi but also "The Grandfather of Texas." In 1821 Moses Austin traveled to San Antonio where he received the first American grant for a colony in Texas. Upon his return he was exposed to severe hardships and became ill. He died 10 June 1821 in St. Francois County and was originally buried at Hazel Run.

In 1828 his body was disinterred and reburied in the Potosi City Cemetery. During the transfer it was discovered that Austin's coffin was completely rotten but his body was perfectly preserved except for his nose and some of his fingers.

After his re-interment word got around about his body being petrified and the grave and coffin was dug up and opened by parties unknown. Once again Moses Austin was re-interred. Eventually a stone enclosure was erected over his grave.

After Moses' death his son Stephen took over the project of moving 300 families from Potosi

©-ZIOCK63664

to Texas thereby making Stephen "The Father of Texas." Austin, the capitol of Texas, is named for Stephen Austin.

BODY SNATCHER: But poor old Moses wasn't allowed to rest peacefully just yet. In

Recently Published...

Haints, Haunts & History's Mysteries Of Southeast Missouri

The Author is Esther Ziock Carroll and a Washington Co., Mo. Genealogist/Historian as well as Ghost Hunter, Founder of Ozark Haint Hunters.

Venture into the supernatural world of witches, ghosts, ancient spirits, violent deaths, mysterious happenings & paranormal investigations. Stories & incidents from five southeast Missouri counties: Washington, Jefferson, St. Francois, Franklin, St. Louis County & the City of St. Louis. Background history researched personally by the author (a 45+year genealogist/historian) is also provided on most of the haunted locations.

Story titles for Washington County are: Religious Cult, On Old Legend, Body Snatcher, Flying Teddy Bear, Dead Baby Cries, Haunted Spring, Horrible Murder & Butchery, Ancient Graves Unearthed, Haunted 1790s Building, The Haunting Of Caledonia Wine Cottage, Haunted Mansion, Resurrection, The Howling, Screams In The Night, Washington County Witch, A Message From The Other Side, Mysterious Foot-

Haints, Haunts & History's Mysteries Of Southeast Missouri

Esther Ziock-Carroll

steps, Man Shoots Ghost, Mysterious Stones, Feather Death Crowns, Ouija Board, & more.

Copies may be ordered from CreateSpace or Amazon.com

#Partnering4Health

Tips On Shopping At Farmers Markets: Get More Fresh Produce In Your Diet

Shopping at farmers markets is one way to get delicious and fresh produce you can enjoy at home.

"Getting plenty of fruits and vegetables helps families live healthier lives and reduces the likelihood of chronic disease," said Elaine Auld, CEO of the Society for Public Health Education (SOPHE). "Lack of nutritious foods puts people at high risk

assisting people and communities t live healthier.

A third of the projects are suppor ed through the National WIC Asso ciation (NWA). The American Hea Association, the American Plannin Association and the Directors of Health Promotion & Education, an also involved.

USDA provides federal grants t

1938 Texans tried to steal his body. An undertaker and hearse were sent to Potosi. One morning the undertaker was discovered hacking away at the tomb thinking the body was inside (actually it is down in the ground). However, the law and angry citizens ran the Texas undertaker out of town.

A few weeks later the Governor of Texas sent the Secretary of State to Potosi with a public apology for the incident. Potosians like to brag that we are the only town that ever took on the state of Texas and won!!

Somewhere along the line a tradition started where someone would walk up to Austin's grave and say, "Whatcha doin' down there Moses?" And he says.......nothing.

FLYING TEDDY BEAR: This house is on High Street in Potosi. Back in the 1990's someone opened up a boutique in the home. A friend of mine (now deceased) told me that she (my friend) was going upstairs to look around at the items and antiques for sale when a teddy bear came flying down the steps at her. But when she got upstairs there was no one up there that could've thrown it.

DEAD BABY CRIES: The story that I was told was about a baby who died. It was brought to Potosi to be checked out and the baby was definitely dead. The mother, who was said to be a witch, was in a trance and screamed at the baby and the baby cried even though it was dead. This was witnessed by 20 people.

HAUNTED SPRING: On an 1870s map of Washington County it lists a haunted spring. Supposedly there was a woman who drowned at the spring. Sometimes when there is a storm people claim you can see a woman in a white dress there.

! WARNING !

**Turn the page if you might,
If you think you can stand the fright.
Lock the doors and windows tight,
And don't read this story late at night.**

HORRIBLE MURDER AND BUTCHERY

FIVE PERSONS BRUTALLY MASSACRED

BODIES MUTILATED & BURNED TO CINDERS

This is the <u>true</u> story of the Lapine family who were murdered by Charlie Jolly and John Armstrong in the year 1870. It was considered the most horrible crime ever committed in Washington County and the entire state of Missouri.

THE CRIME: On Monday morning, November 21, 1870, Washington County was shocked beyond description upon discovering that a family of French Creoles - David and Louisa Lapine (a.k.a. Lago) and their child along with Mrs. Lapine's sister, Mary Christopher and her child, were brutally murdered in their cabin one and a half miles north of Potosi near Brushy Mine Diggins'. The horrifying scene of the crime was described as follows:

"A sullen gloom overhangs it like a tragic curtain, and the hollow murmur of the stunted oaks constantly mumbling of things too horrible to tell plainly."

"Over all there hung a sense of fear, A sense of mystery the spirit daunted;

That said as plain as whisper on the ear,
The place is haunted."

What was left of the Lapine family was gathered and put in a box, brought to Potosi and buried in the city cemetery. Sheriff Clarke immediately began an investigation which quickly determined the perpetrators of the heinous crime. Upon questioning the citizens of the neighborhood, witnesses were located. Leon Jolly stated that his brother, Charles Jolly, and his cousin, John Armstrong (also Creoles) were the murderers. John Jolly (brother of Leon and Charley) and others also testified as to what they were told after the crime. Their combined stories are given as follows:

On Saturday night, November 19th, after indulging in whiskey, Leon and Charley Jolly and John Armstrong went to the Lapine cabin at about midnight. Leon, age 14, who was not permitted to enter the cabin, held a jug of whiskey and watched through a crack in the cabin wall. John Armstrong, who was carrying an ax, burst open the front door. The Lapine family was all asleep. Charley shot Davey four times then shot Mary in the head. Louisa was then around him holding to his coattail and he knocked her in the head with his fist then shot her. John Armstrong chopped Davey's head off then chopped the women and children in the head with the ax. The two fiends then set fire to the cabin, burning the mutilated bodies beyond recognition. With blood still on their hands and clothing, they returned to John Jolly's home for breakfast.

The murderers did not flee the area until Monday when the crime was discovered. Sheriff Clarke quickly organized a posse that set off in vigorous pursuit. The chase led to Jefferson County where four citizens apprehended the criminals as they sat at supper at the Bellagantha Lucas house. They were given to the posse and returned to Potosi.

On November 26th, an attempt was made to lynch the prisoners by outraged citizens.

About 12:30 at night a mob of 75 people appeared in front of the jail, a one story brick structure about fifteen feet north of the courthouse (the present courthouse stands on the same site.) The sheriff and four other men were stationed on the second floor of the courthouse armed with revolvers and double barreled shotguns. The angry mob was ordered to disperse or be fired upon, but they kept yelling, "Keys! Keys!" and howling and shouting. After one warning shot in the air the sheriff and men fired indiscriminately down at the crowd, sending them fleeing in all directions. A young man named Mainwaring was killed and six or seven others were wounded.

THE TRIAL: The trial began at Potosi Wednesday, December 21, 1870, at 10:00 A.M. with J. Brady appointed as defense council. For the prosecution, G. Reynolds was assisted by Wm. Relfe. The jurors were: Wm. Evens (foreman), D.W. Proffit, S. Philpot, B.S. Dicus, R.H. Dickey, L. Hope, J.P. Blount, R.P. Martin, J. Wilson, P. Wood, J.A. Pinson, and

J.W. Garret. Two of the jurors, Brad Dicus and Robert Dickey, were my ancestors. Both defendants pleaded "not guilty" with John Armstrong claiming he was not present at the Lapine cabin the night of the murders.

The case was presented throughout the day with testimony given by various witnesses including members of the defendants' own family. No family members testified on their behalf or even attended the trial except those ordered to do so by the court. The proceedings closed at 10:30 P.M. It took the jury 10 minutes to return with a verdict of "GUILTY."

The next day the prisoners were sentenced to be hanged. A deathlike silence reigned in the courtroom during the pronouncement of the sentences. Charles Jolly received his sentence with stoicism and made no reply. John Armstrong, however, received his sentence with agitation and replied in broken sentences, still denying his guilt and claiming he was not present at the cabin the night of the murders. The judge solemnly closed the sentencing with the invocation, "May God have mercy on your soul."

The prisoners were then remanded to jail in St. Louis owing to the fact that the county jail had been condemned as unfit for human habitation. After the courtroom cleared of observers the following anonymously written poem was found in the rubbish on the floor:

Charles Jolly, Armstrong known as John,
Through their great trial just have gone.

The jury did a solemn task
And rendered all the State could ask

But could the law have given more,
The jury would have granted sure.

For greater crime was never done
Beneath the rolling of the sun

The children, sister, husband, wife
Were all submitted to the knife

Or other instrument of death
That took away all of their breath

To shoot, and cut, and kill and burn
To make a home a lonely urn

Great God! how boson burn and swell
To know such monsters out of Hell

The sentences next, a few days given
That they may pray and think of Heaven

Then we will live in the brightest hope
That they will feel the tightening rope

And others learn from their example
The power of law so great and ample

When the last rites have been performed
By solemn law, with virtue crowned

Then we may sleep from night to night,
With full conviction all is right.

THE EXECUTION: Actual headlines from the "Missouri Republican" out of St. Louis: "The Gallows Tree", "Double Execution at Potosi", "A Gala Day in a Rural Region", "Ghastly Scenes and Exciting Incidents".

Friday, January 27th, 1871 - Potosi bustled with activity and excitement, hotels and streets were crowded as hundreds of people of all ages - men, women and even children - dressed in holiday attire, came from as far as 30 miles away to witness the execution. One farmer, who was over 80 years old, walked 20 miles through the snow to be present at this historic occasion.

Charles Jolly and John Armstrong were returned from St. Louis by train. They were held at the courthouse while ropes were placed and readied on the gallows which had been erected on the north side of the courthouse near the jail. This would be the first "legal" execution to be held in Washington County. Prior to it only lynchings had occurred.

While waiting for the clergy to arrive the impatient crowd, eager to see the prisoners, began to shout, "Bring them out! Bring them out!" Four clergymen attended the prisoners, two from St. Louis and Rev.'s Brennan and Manning from Potosi.

Finally, at 1:40 P.M. the prisoners were taken to the gallows and Sheriff Clarke read the execution warrant with evident emotion. After the priests spoke with the prisoners, Father O'Reilly stepped to the front of the platform and addressed the crowd: "The men here present and now to be executed, have been condemned judicially by the court of this county, whether tried correctly or not, it is not for me to say. They only wish to say that they desire to plead neither guilty nor not guilty. If they are guilty, God knows it. If they are not guilty, God knows it. The evidence seems to say that they are, and in the eyes of the law they are guilty and worthy of death. But they desire to die pleading neither one way or the other."

Deputy Breckenridge and his assistant then put black caps over the faces of the prisoners and nooses were placed in position, being drawn so tight as to almost choke them.

Farewells were said. Armstrong trembled slightly.

At 2:08 the order was given, "Now." The trap was opened and both dropped through. Jolly's head was almost severed from his body. Armstrong, however, dropped lower with his toes barely scraping the ground. His noose had come partially untied and he slowly strangled.

At 2:13 Dr. Bell pronounced both men dead. They are buried in the Catholic cemetery. No motive was ever determined for their vicious and bloody crime although some people believed it to be a dispute over a tiff mining claim.

In the 1900s, during the summer, two people were at the location of this horrible crime. One of them got goose bumps all over her body and was cold to the touch. She informed her companion that they must leave the area immediately as there was something going on there that wasn't right. Over the years the property has been strip-mined and is now a cow pasture. I was told there may be a pond where the cabin used to be.

MURDER AT MIDNIGHT

(Formerly titled Haunted Halloween)
By: Esther M. Ziock Carroll

This tale is bloody and brutal but true,
On a lonely night it could frighten you.
So lock the doors and windows tight,
And don't read this story late at night.

Five sleeping victims in 1870,
Would be violently sent to eternity.
The murderers hasten down a darkened path,
So intent to vent their wrath.

At midnight the evil witching hour,
Is when these monsters wield their power.
Beating, shooting, chopping with an ax,
In depravity they were not lax.

One victim awoke and tried to fight,
Struggled she did with all her might.
But the battle she waged was all in vain,
She lost her life in fear and pain.

This horrible crime was the worst one ever,
As the husband's head they did sever.
And the tiny children they did cry,
When they saw it was time to die.

Blood was splattered everywhere,
Terror reigned but they did not care.
In a drunken, fevered, frenzied din,
The fiends committed unforgivable sin.

Then the lonely cabin was set ablaze,
Creating an eerie, glowing haze.
Returning home for their morning meal,
No remorse did the murderers feel.

The criminals tried to flee from the law,
Leaving the county behind in shock and awe.
But they were caught 'n tried 'n hung up high,
Now it was their turn to suffer and die!

So visit Brushy Run late at night,
If you think you can stand the fright.
Maybe you'll hear a desperate scream,
Is it real or just a dream?

Is that a ghostly figure you see,
Lurking by an old oak tree?

Could their spirits travel the mists of time,
And still be near Brushy Run mine?

ANCIENT GRAVES UNEARTHED: From –
"The Independent Journal" 1925: - Alex
Cordia, foreman of the group excavating for
Potosi's sewerage system, reports that as the
men were cutting the ditch from Hwy. 8
through the A.H. Long property to Breton
Street the excavation ran into four shallow
graves situated just outside the cemetery
fence. Mr. Cordia said the graves were
evidently of ancient construction as there was
no evidence of any coffins. No nails, buttons
or other indications of burial equipment. The
graves, Mr. Cordia stated, were not more than
three feet deep and about 20 inches wide.
They had a scooped out appearance, the
bones resting on the loose porous rock of the
shallow bottoms. The bones were carefully
collected and placed in boxes and re-interred
in the same excavations from which they were

removed. The graves were in a straight line but outside the cemetery enclosure, leading the men to conclude that at some former time the fence had been set in, or that the graves had been placed outside. They were made either before the times of coffins or hastily interred without benefit of coffin; however the entire absence of any foreign material led Mr. Cordia to conclude that the graves were made in the times of winding sheets.

SANDY'S GHOST: Our beloved dog, Sandy, died in 1996. She had always slept on the floor by my side of the bed. Anytime I got up during the night to go to the bathroom she would always escort me there by walking next to me on my right side and I could always smell her doggy odor as we walked.

It was in the first few months after she died that I got up one night for my usual bathroom trip and I could smell her doggy odor following beside me and I could just sense that she was there. This happened one more time in the next few months but the odor wasn't as strong and it didn't last as long. Then it never happened again. I truly believe she came to visit us and to let us know that she is alright. But I still miss her very much.

APPARITION: The Clara Hall house was built in the 1830s by relatives of Daniel Dunklin who was Washington County's second sheriff and Missouri's fifth governor. Written on the wall in an upstairs room were the words, "I spent the day in the berry patch with Alice, July 23, 1844." An apparition was seen in this home. Unfortunately this house burned down in the 1990s.

BLACK SHADOW FIGURE: The occupant of a house was awakened one night by a black shadowy figure on top of him choking him. When he broke free it was gone. Another time an apparition was seen in the hallway and quickly disappeared into the living room.

Unfortunately this house was later torn down.

UNEXPLAINABLE OCCURANCES: James Long built this beautiful Victorian style house in Potosi circa 1865 and the grounds occupied the entire block on Mine, Pine and Clark Streets, with a stable and carriage house on the rear lots. The Long-Banta house has approximately 10 rooms not including the entrance hall, basement and attic. It is still furnished with many of the Long family's original furniture.

At least five family members are known to have died in the house over the years. James died in 1916 and is buried in the Presbyterian Cemetery on Breton Street almost directly across the street from his home. It is said that his ghost haunts the home.

People have also reported strange unexplainable noises occurring in the house, and being touched when no one else was there. A child has been seen several times peering out one of the windows when no one was occupying the house.

During a ghost tour I snapped a picture of someone who walked by the front door on the

outside during a haunted tour near Halloween. However when I up loaded it to my computer the image that showed up looks nothing like that person. It looks as though this "person" dressed all in black is entering the house and not just walking by.

When I took a picture of the stairway into the basement (which was the basement from a previous home) I had a very strong feeling/sensation of someone or something standing about midway down the steps although nothing showed up in the picture. I also get that feeling every time I look at that picture.

In another picture, taken in an upstairs room above the kitchen, I saw a large reddish-orange glowing orb through the viewfinder in my camera about a second BEFORE the flash. It was above the stairwell but disappointingly it did not show up in the photo.

In one of the upstairs bedrooms a visitor sensed an unwelcome presence and thought she saw the edge of one of the pillow cases move. Orbs have also been photographed in the house.

AIN'T NO HAINT GONNA RUN ME OFF! Some years ago when I was still with the local historical society and was still a volunteer tour guide for some of the historic buildings in Potosi an incident occurred one Sunday afternoon. Gene and I were scheduled to staff the Banta House in Potosi as tour guides. We obtained a key and at the designated time unlocked and opened the house for tours. No tourists had yet arrived so we were planning on sitting on the nice shady front porch for the afternoon waiting for any tourists that might want to take a tour.

This big, beautiful Victorian style home was built in the 1860's over an old, dingy stone cellar or basement which had been the cellar to a previous house on that same lot. The Banta House has several large rooms on the first and second floors and a small stairway leading from the trunk room upstairs to a dusty, spooky old attic. The house is furnished with beautiful antique beds, chairs, large wardrobes, steamer trunks and other furniture.

Over the more than 130 years of the home's existence at least five family members died in the house. The Banta house is rumored to be haunted so anytime I gave a tour through the house I always mentioned this in the tour dissertation. I thought it kind of added a bit of mystery to the place and the tourists seemed to enjoy the tour more, sometimes even making humorous comments about bodies in the trunks, etc.

Well, after Gene and I opened the house that day Gene started putting some chairs on the front porch while I went waaaaaaaay to the back of the house to the kitchen to see if there were any sodas in the fridge. In the kitchen there is the steep, narrow enclosed stairway which comes down from what used to be the maid's room upstairs. I had only been in the kitchen a few minutes when I heard the distinct sound of slow, heavy footsteps coming down that stairway. Suddenly I felt a kind of adrenalin surge go through my body but I couldn't run – I was curiously frozen to the spot where I was standing. I couldn't seem to do anything except stand and stare at that stairway wall and think, "OH, CRAP!! SOMETHING IS COMING DOWN THOSE STAIRS!!" My heart began pounding louder and louder as the footsteps came closer to the bottom of the stairs. I seemed to almost stop breathing as my eyes focused on that stairway door waiting for it to open. I vaguely remember thinking that now would be a good time to run, but still my feet just wouldn't move! Then with an eerie creak the door slowly began to swing open and then I saw.....................

Gene. Yep, it was my husband! I had thought he was still out on the front porch but he had gone up the stairway at the front of the house to check out the upstairs and make sure everything was all right. Because the house is so big I had not heard him go up those front steps but I sure heard him when he came down the back ones! When he opened the stairway door and I saw it was him and not a "haint" I couldn't help but laugh, laugh, laugh at myself for reacting the way I did! Gene innocently stepped into the kitchen, looked at me real bewildered and said, "What the hell is so funny?" Now he knows - and so do you.

HISTORY OF SWEET MEMORIES: I participated in several investigations here. My cousin is the owner of this beautiful antebellum home from which she operates a catering business called Sweet Memories. It is in Potosi's historic district on Breton Street. It was built in the 1800's and still maintains its historic charm.

It is unknown who the original builder of the home was or when, specifically, it was built.

There used to be a small house in the back,

which is no longer there, that was referred to by old-timers as the "slave house." However, the ownership history of the land goes back to 1798. It was part of the land that Moses Austin acquired in Spanish Grant #430.

In 1814 Austin deeded 40 acres to the county commissioners, Benjamin Elliott, Martin Ruggles, and Lionel Browne, for the establishment of a county seat. John Rice Jones donated 10 acres however he later rescinded his acreage. The land was divided into lots and sold. The next record of the property is 1845 when Charity and Samuel Harrison sold to James Lucas.

In 1869 James A. Shields, commissioner for Washington County, sold to Garrett I. Van Allen, who was the prosecuting Attorney of Washington County. Harriett, Mr. Van Allen's wife, died in 1871. This death occurred while the Van Allen family was living in this house. Harriett is buried just down the street in the Presbyterian Cemetery.

In 1887 James and Elizabeth Homan were the next owners of the house. James had been a steamboat pilot since the age of 18, navigating the lower Mississippi from St. Louis to New Orleans. It is said that he made nearly 1,100 trips between the two points.

In 1893 Francis Connelly, a merchant, purchased the home and lived there for 34 years. The next owners were Al and Joyce Weiss who lived in the house for 42 years. Joyce operated a beauty shop there.

SWEET HAUNTED MEMORIES: David and Cindy Merx bought the house from John More in 2002. During the refurbishing they began to notice odd occurrences which amplified over time. They eventually concluded that the home was haunted.

The staff of Sweet Memories affectionately calls their ghost "Harriet" as they believe it may be the ghost of Harriet Van Allen who lived in the house from 1869 until she met an untimely demise in 1871 at the age of 44.

Harriet is not a malicious ghost but has been a bit unnerving at times. Some of her mischievous antics include: knocking things off the walls or shelves, opening and closing doors, or putting in a glimpse of an appearance. Sometimes small objects get rearranged. One time a noodle came flying through the air in the kitchen and landed on the floor. Since the staff wasn't cooking noodles that day they have no clue where the noodle came from. Another time near Halloween a small scarecrow table decoration fell over all on it's own at an unoccupied table while Cindy was reciting stories about Harriet to Parkland Paranormal that was there to investigate. This occurrence was witnessed by six people, including my husband Gene Carroll.

One day Harriet did not like a table cloth that had been put on one of the tables and kept removing it and putting it on the floor while the staff was busy in the kitchen. After four or five times replacing the table cloth Cindy told them that apparently Harriet didn't like it and to put a different table cloth on the table. That one stayed on.

Another time the upstairs tenant asked Cindy if she had been there late the night before as they had smelled cookies baking all night. She had not been there the night before. One time the staff was discussing ghosts and one of them stated how they didn't believe in ghosts. Right at that moment a can of Mandarin oranges flew out of the open kitchen cabinet and landed directly at the skeptic's feet.

Another time a shadow person was observed running through the dining room. And while the house was unoccupied an employee stopped by to check on something. After she came in the front door she saw a woman on the stairway dressed in 1800s clothing. The employee made a hasty exit from the building. Several paranormal groups have done investigations here.

HISTORY OF THE CALEDONIA WINE COTTAGE: The Wine Cottage is a beautiful three story antebellum home located in historic Caledonia. Caledonia, founded in 1819, is a quaint little village in the scenic Bellevue Valley of Washington County.

Upon entering the Cottage, which is listed on the National Register of Historic Places, visitors will notice a continuous three-story walnut stairway believed to be the only staircase of its kind in the Ozarks. Local legend claims that Jacob Fisher built the house in 1824. It served as a stage stop, tavern and inn. The stage would drive up a stone road to the inn to let the passengers off. Some of these stones are still here today and serve as the foundation for the front steps of the Wine Cottage.

The three-story structure originally had 12 rooms, and a dirt floor basement, with separate quarters in the back for slaves. The slaves were allegedly jointly owned by Jacob Fisher and the families on both sides of the building.

There were supposedly tunnels connecting all three buildings, which the slaves used to go from one home to another. One tunnel went under what is now Hwy. 21, coming out by the creek where the slaves went out to work in the fields.

It was in the middle tunnel that led to the creek

that Mr. Fisher brutally and mercilessly beat one of his female slaves to death with a stick in 1829. Her name was Patience and her death has been documented. There was a large bruise on her right hip, a cut above her right eye, her left ear was smashed and partly torn off, and her neck and both arms were broken.

Although it was legally permissible at that time to whip one's slaves, killing them was in violation of the law. However, no legal action was taken against Fisher. But, due to the extreme disapproval of the community about his vicious actions he removed himself from Washington County.

The Cottage has been a witness to many events over the years. In the 1830s B. B. Cannon's contingent of the Trail of Tears passed through Caledonia.

Prior to the Civil War, the tunnels beneath the wine cottage were supposedly used as an underground railroad to help move runaway slaves further north. There is now a concrete slab in the basement covering the entrance to these tunnels.

During the Civil War, after a major battle at Ft. Davidson in Pilot Knob in Iron County, the Union soldiers passed through Caledonia during their northern retreat while being pursued by Gen. Sterling Price's Confederate army.

The Wine Cottage served as a hospital for sick and wounded soldiers, both Union and Confederate. The "Quarantine Room" on the third floor of the Cottage still has the small window in the door where food was passed through to the sick and contagious soldiers. When the Confederate soldiers were well enough, they became prisoners of war and were kept locked in the basement with bars on the windows. These bars are still here today. Some of the soldiers died in this building and were buried in the nearby Bellevue Presbyterian Cemetery where there is a tombstone in their memory.

The Wine Cottage has had many owners over the years. The property that Caledonia now occupies was acquired in 1804 in a Spanish Grant by Miles Goforth who was a Revolutionary War Soldier from the state of Virginia. He came to Washington County from Tennessee. Miles taught the first school in Bellevue Valley and also served as constable of Bellevue Township.

William Buford, a wealthy slave owner, came to Missouri in 1812 and settled in Bellevue Valley. Buford Mountain on the east side of the Valley is named after him and is the third highest mountain in Missouri.

In 1815 Buford purchased 440 acres of the Goforth grant, which included the land that would eventually become the town of Caledonia.

Alexander Craighead was of Scottish descent and came to Missouri from Tennessee. He purchased land from William Buford and, circa 1818, platted the town of Caledonia and the lots were sold at auction. He said whoever purchased the first lot could name the town. He himself purchased the first lot and named the town Caledonia.

William Buford purchased the half acre Lot #18 at the auction which is the lot that the Wine Cottage now occupies. Buford owned the lot for three years before selling it to Jacob Fisher in 1822.

Jacob Fisher purchased Lot #18 from William Buford in 1822 and owned it for five years. He allegedly built the house that is now the Wine Cottage as a stage stop, tavern and inn.

In November 1827, Fisher sold lot 18 along with its adjoining Lot 7 and Lots 45 and 54, "together with all houses, out houses and other improvements" for $1,000.

Augustus Jones purchased Lot 18 from Jacob Fisher in 1827 and owned the lot for eleven years. During his lifetime, Augustus was a personal friend of President Andrew Jackson, was a deputy sheriff of Washington County, and represented the county in the state legislature. He participated in a number of duels, served in the War of 1812, the Mexican War and was Major General of the Missouri State Militia. In 1829, he platted the Jones Addition to the town of Potosi. He was a high ranking freemason for nearly 70 years. Augustus Jones had 5 step children and 18 children of his own by three wives. Mr. Jones moved to Texas in 1851 and died in that state at the age of 90 years.

James S. Evens purchased Lot 18 from Augustus Jones in 1838 and owned it for five years. Mr. Evans was a supporter of all the churches in the area, especially the Bellevue Collegiate Institute. He was also a member of the Masonic Fraternity. He had very little formal education, having been home-schooled by his father. With hard work and good management, he became one of the wealthier men of this county. After building a lead furnace at Old Mines, he came to Bellevue Valley in 1837 and opened a store at Caledonia. To his list of accomplishments he added a blacksmith shop, a second store, a sawmill, and the first steam flourmill in the Valley. However, The War Of The Rebellion took nearly everything leaving he and his family almost destitute. During the war he had been taken prisoner and barely escaped with his life.

Pleasant McDonald bought Lot 18 that he then occupied from James S. Evens in 1843 and owned it for four years. Mr. McDonald came to Washington County, Missouri, in 1841 / 1842.

Chastain Hicks, a slave owner, occupied Lot 18 in 1847 and in that same year purchased the lot from Sarah Ann and Pleasant McDonald. Mr. Hicks owned the lot for twenty years. Mr. Hicks was an early settler in this county, having come here as a child with his parents. According to one report: "During the Civil War he was a strong Union man. When he married his first wife he had nothing.

However he worked hard at blacksmithing and farming and at the time of his death in 1888 he was one of the more well-to-do farmers in the community with many friends."

William S. Relfe purchased a half interest of Lot 18 (with other property) "at the sale of lands delinquent for taxes for the year 1866 and former years said sale being on the 7th and 8th days of October, 1867." (Strangely, the over due tax statement was issued to Jacob Fisher who had sold the property in 1827.) Relfe owned the lot for one month. He graduated Arcadia College and taught there for one year. He studied law and was admitted to the Bar in 1865. He was prosecuting attorney of Washington County from 1872–1874. Elected to the legislature in 1874, he served on several committees. In 1877, he was appointed superintendant of the insurance department for the state of Missouri. He eventually settled in St. Louis and was regarded as one of the most honorable and industrious members of the St. Louis Bar. He was also a member of the Legion of Honor and the Knights Templars and was secretary of Masonic Mutual Benefit Society.

James A. Shields also purchased a half interest of Lot 18 (with other property.) He was commissioner for Washington County and abstractor of titles.

Lucius Judson purchased William S. Relfe's half interest in Lot 18 (with other property) on 16 November, 1867.

James R. Arnold (by trustee) sold the property in 1876. Mr. Arnold had come to Missouri in the 1850s.

William Crommer acquired Lot 18 in 1876 and owned it for 13 years before selling it to the Eatons in 1889.

Mollie and Jesse L. Eaton were the next owners. Jesse was the son of Ollie Ramsey and Dr. John A. Eaton. Jesse had come to Caledonia in 1887. He was a physician, a Mason, and a member of A.O.U.W. Jesse served as a Democrat representative with the Missouri Legislature. He was married to Mollie

S. Maxwell.

Joseph Cosby Crenshaw, a former slave owner, moved to Caledonia in 1850 from Charleston, Missouri so his children could attend the Bellevue Collegiate Institute. He purchased the property in 1890 from the Eatons. His wife Rachel Ann Lusk Marbury kept roomers and boarders who also attended the Bellevue Collegiate Institute.

R.A. Crenshaw, according to an 1895 deed: "wife of Joseph Crenshaw to Jos. C. Crenshaw...........in consideration of love and affection ....and further consideration of $400 to her paid."

J.C. Crenshaw and R.A. Crenshaw to William C. Crenshaw, according to an 1897 deed: "in consideration of love and affection and the sum of $1.00 to him paid...........R.A. Crenshaw for and during her natural life time with remainder in fee to the said William C. Crenshaw."

William Crenshaw was a dentist and son of

Joseph Crenshaw and became owner of the property. He married Bessie Pearl Ramsey in 1900 and they later moved to St. Louis. In 1922, their daughter, Mildred Mary, and her husband William Thomas Coghill made the Cottage their home. In 1926, the Crenshaws sold the property to J.M. and Laura Ramsey.

Laura and James Ramsey and Isla & William M. McKeehn 1931 deed........in consideration of $100 and other valuable consideration........all of Lot 18.....together with the improvements thereon.........

McKeehn and wife to J.M. Ramsey, Lot 18 in Caledonia. 1931 deed.

William T. Ramsey and Hallie (Martin) Ramsey became the owners of the Cottage in 1945 and this house was commonly known as "The Ramsey House." During the Ramseys' ownership of the home, the residence was placed on the National Register of Historic Places. Both Mr. and Mrs. Ramsey died here.

The Cottage was also owned by Charles and Lisa Medlock then by Dale and Sandra Brown who operated it as Bellevue Antiques and Arts.

In 2006 Almeta "Pepper" Carpenter and Dave Buis purchased the house from Michael and Donna Bond. After renovations Pepper and Dave opened it in 2007 as the Caledonia Wine Cottage Bed and Breakfast. It was during the refurbishing that things took a turn to the mysterious and unexplainable.........

THE HAUNTING OF THE CALEDONIA WINE COTTAGE: When the renovation began in 2006, occupants of The Wine Cottage began experiencing numerous supernatural occurrences. It all began with the opening up of the old slave quarters.

Unexplained incidents began happening periodically through-out the entire house. People often hear the friendly voice of an elderly woman saying "Hello" on the first floor of The Cottage. And one family who brought their three-year-old son here numerous times says that he often waves at an unseen person in the corner of the dining room.

There have been instances when corks have unexpectedly shot out of wine bottles. Even the family dog was affected – he was observed looking curiously at areas where nothing was seen by others.

Another child whose family stayed in the Bed and Breakfast rooms on the third floor met a female playmate named "Erica" while staying at The Cottage when there were no other children staying there at the time.

In the Quarantine Room a door opened and closed on its own and a small rocking chair began rocking with no one in it. Also a wrist watch of one occupant that was laying on a small table was violently thrown across the room to the floor.

In the room across the hall from the Quarantine Room the occupants clothing, specifically a t-shirt, was re-arranged while they slept. An employee at the Cottage told of an incident involving a customer who was sitting outside on the deck-patio by the air conditioner. When the employee came back out to bring the lady and her husband their order, they had moved away from the air conditioner to the other side of the deck. When the employee asked them why they moved the woman hesitatingly said that she was clairvoyant and sensitive to spirits, and while sitting close to the air conditioner she had a very strong feeling of a spooky voice saying, "Emily is here." The employee asked her if she was sure she didn't mean "Erica," as we know we have an Erica. The woman said that the voice definitely stated "Emily."

After the couple finished eating, they came inside to look around. The woman went upstairs to the 3rd floor but she would not go into the Quarantine Room, as she sensed that it was just plain evil.

Mysterious footsteps have been heard in the Cottage by people at varying times along with voices when no one else was there. Objects have been thrown or dropped by unseen forces. A shadow figure of what is believed to be a Civil War soldier has been observed on several occasions. Subsequently several paranormal groups have conducted investigations at The Cottage one of which was covered by the <u>Daily Journal</u> a St. Francois County newspaper.

When I was with one group and we were in the Quarantine Room my laser thermometer detected a cold spot on the wall over the bed. Also my photograph of the wall showed an unexplained white anomaly right next to where the cold spot was.

While I was doing a lone EVP session in the dining room, whispers that could not be heard during the session, were on the voice recorder when played back but it was unclear what was being said. However one barely audible whisper says "Don't go" just a few seconds before the assistant manager loudly says, "Bye Bye!" to those investigators in the kitchen as she leaves for the evening.

While the men of one of the paranormal groups were conducting an EVP session in the kitchen, someone noticed that the small green light on the chest freezer was flickering frantically and thought perhaps a spirit was trying to communicate by way of the light. When questions were asked of the light it responded by flashing once for yes and twice for no. However, when I entered the kitchen, the light went off and refused to communicate further. The question was then asked about the light not wanting to communicate because there was a woman in the room. It still didn't respond. Then when I announced that I was leaving the room and stepped out of the kitchen the light immediately came back on and stayed steadily on but refused to respond to anymore questions. Even though that spirit didn't like me it didn't have to be so rude!

While I was standing alone in the dark wine room trying to decide where I wanted to go next I saw a red light moving towards me.

Well, I let out a shriek that would make a banshee jealous! Turned out it was one of the other investigators with his ghost detector.

In 2016 the Wine Cottage was purchased by Roger and Pamela Allen and reopened as Twelve Mile Creek Emporium, Wine Cottage and Bed and Breakfast. Pamela gave me a tour of the place and I got to see the slave quarters for the first time. While going up the stairs to the quarters I thought I saw out of the corner of my eye a person dressed in black standing toward the back of the room. However, when I got up to the room there was no one there.

HAUNTED MANSION: Robert Bust, of English birth, located in Washington County, Missouri, in 1855. In 1865 Mr. Bust was married to Miss Lucy McGready, a daughter of Dr. James H. and Mary Ann (McClanahan) McGready, who were among the early settlers of Washington County. They became the parents of eight children. Robert Bust died 8 November 1897.

The Bust Mansion was built in the 1800's. Very little is left of what was once a very beautiful home that has quite a reputation for being

haunted. One source says that there was a baby who was either killed or died in front of the fireplace and there have been sightings of a baby in or near the fireplace in the home. There may be ghosts of slaves there too.

An anonymous source tells that one time they saw a very large (human size) black bat on the roof. It was there for about a minute and then vanished. Eight people witnessed this phenomenon at the same time.

Another time this Anonymous, along with a friend, were walking near the mansion when a large tree (approximately 2-3 feet in diameter) fell just a few feet in front of them. They said you could feel the ground shake when it crashed down. They ran away screaming. When they went back about 20 minutes later to try and determine what had caused the tree to fall it wasn't there!

HAUNTED 1790s BUILDING: This is allegedly the oldest structure still standing in Washington County. This building has been a witness to many people and events. Most were never written down and have been lost forever. The Austin-Milam-Lucas Store is believed to date back to 1798 and was built by Moses Austin. A few hundred feet away was Moses Austin's home Durham Hall which burned in 1871.

In 1802 thirty Indians attacked Mine Au Breton with intentions of killing the Americans and plundering Austin's home and store. There was one person killed and one woman kidnapped. It is unknown at this time who she was or what became of her – another history mystery.

One well known event, however, was the "Trail of Tears" in 1838. One of the routes came through Washington County and the Indians

purchased supplies from this store. It was also here during the Civil War when Gen. Sterling Price's Confederate Army invaded Potosi in 1864.

A suicide was committed in the building in

1932. The person was F.J. Flynn a cashier at a local bank. At the time of the suicide, the store was a private residence. Mr. Flynn, who was in poor health, shot himself in an upstairs room. He was found by his sister and niece.

Inside the house people have experienced odd odors as well as lights and appliances turning on and off on their own when this was once an apartment building. Cold spots have been detected as well as strange noises. People on the outside of the building have observed a shadow figure passing by an upstairs window and have reported seeing the shadow of a man looking out from the window in the room where the suicide occurred.

During an investigation the batteries of one investigator went dead even though they were brand new. I ventured upstairs by myself but quickly came back down as I had seen someone standing in one of the rooms even though there was supposed to be no one else up there. It turned out to be just a mannequin.

RESURRECTION: Years ago we planted a Butterfly Bush in our back yard but it eventually died. It was dead for several years. One could break some of the wood from it and it was dry and brittle. Then one summer day Gene decided to finally cut it completely down. When he came back into the house he said, "You're not going to believe this." We went outside to see the bush and it had fresh little leaves on it. It had come back to life and was growing again.

ANOTHER RESURRECTION: Some friends of ours had a cute little beagle dog that was accidently hit and killed. The little dog laid in their yard for about 20 minutes while they prepared to bury it. When they went to bury him all of a sudden it jumped up and began running around as if nothing had happened.

THE HOWLING: Between an old cemetery and Tiff Road is a site that Gene and I found where stones were placed as if outlining several graves. An archeologist acquaintance thought it might be Indian graves. Also many years ago I saw a solid white wolf near this area. Years later the nearby resident heard an extremely forlorn howling in the woods as if a dog were sick, injured or dying. Myself and this person went to where the sound had been coming from but never found any incapacitated animal.

SCREAMS IN THE NIGHT: When my step-father, Rudy Foree, lived on John Smith Rd. in the 1980's there was a large spring-fed pond in his front yard. One time at about 3:00 in the morning Rudy heard someone screaming outside at the pond. He went to the front door and turned the outside lights on but no one was there. Later he found out that someone had drowned in the pond at one time.

STRANGE LIGHTS: Due to the location of this property being confidential not all facts can be disclosed. This was an outdoor investigation. The property owner, family, and others have experienced strange lights in the area and have sighted a ghost numerous times. The ghost has even spoken to them. I photographed some orbs at this site but due to very high humidity they may have been moisture orbs. Although I did not experience it two other investigators said the ghost detector did respond in the field indicating the presence of a ghost.

STRANGE RED MIST: One night, I think it was back in the 1980s, there were reports coming in from all over southeast Missouri about patches of strange red mists being sighted. I saw one at the end of our house from our bedroom window. I went outside to get a better look. It looked really weird as it slowly floated passed the house and disappeared down the hill. The mist was on the television news. They said it was nothing to worry about and was some kind of weather phenomenon.

WASHINGTON COUNTY WITCH: There was

a woman struck by lightning at Long's Store in Cadet next to the depot and it did not hurt her. It was a clear day and several people there witnessed it. The word was that she was a witch and they can get struck by lightning and it doesn't hurt them. She got struck three times and lived to a ripe old age.

MYSTERIOUS BONES: The bones of a woman supposed to have burned were found at Bone Hollow Lead Mine two and a half miles southwest of Cruise. It is unknown at this time the circumstances of her death. Another history mystery.

HAUNTED GRAVE: This Civil War soldier is buried where he fell. It has been said that sometimes at night one can see his ghost crossing the road by his grave. Local people take very good care of his grave. There is supposedly a couple of more Civil War graves

in the area but their exact location is no longer known. There used to be a sign on the post which stated the following:

> Behold ye people passing by,
> As you are now, so once was I.
> As I am now, you too will be,
> Prepare yourself to follow me.

OLD HAUNTED HOME: I have a personal connection to this home but due to the confidential location not all facts can be disclosed.

The grounds of this location are said to be haunted as well as the house. It is possible that as many as five people or more may have died in the home over the years. It is believed to have been built circa 1855 –1856. One odd thing about the home is that the logs are hewn on the outside of the house but not on the inside. On the inside they still have the bark on them. For most old log homes it is the opposite – the hewn part is on the inside and

the bark is still left on the outside of the log. Don't know why it was built this way.

When I was taking pictures around the property I noticed later after downloading the pictures there was the strange transparent figure of a man in the backyard. And there was no one standing there at the time I took the picture and the only other person on the property was my husband and he was in the house.

The original sections of the house consist of two rooms downstairs, and two rooms upstairs. In the hallway there is an enclosed staircase. Other rooms have been added over the years.

One time when my husband, who is a retired fire fighter, was there alone the smoke detector in the downstairs hallway began sounding and kept sounding when there was no fire or smoke anywhere in the home. He took it apart and cleaned it then placed it in it's spot on the wall in the hallway. It started sounding again and would not stop. It finally had to be dismantled. A paranormal group that I was familiar with said that spirits can manipulate smoke detectors.

Another time when I was there alone in the smaller room upstairs a metal detector that had been leaning up against the wall since forever suddenly fell over crashing to the floor without being touched.

And an odd thing about this room was that there was a sliding bolt lock on the door – but it was on the outside of the door in the hallway. Most doors lock on the inside in order to keep people out. But this lock was on the outside as if to keep someone in. When I was finished in this room I locked the bolt lock. The next time I visited this house that lock had been unlocked even though no one else had been there.

Following are various incidents I was told about the house: A previous tenant died and was cremated and his ashes were scattered over the grounds. It is said that his ghost haunts the property. The wife of a former owner of the property just disappeared. No one ever knew what happened to her. And mysterious footsteps have been heard on the stairway in middle of the night, a ghostly mist or form was seen floating down the downstairs hallway and disappeared into the bathroom, visitors who were on the porch heard a voice in the house when the house was unoccupied, bedroom light comes on all by itself, also strange sounds can be heard from the kitchen as if someone is rummaging around looking for something. Living room curtains get pulled back by themselves as if someone is looking out the window, living room tv turns on all by itself, there is a sound of plastic hangers clacking together in a closet, the smell of different odors that can't be accounted for such as root beer when no one is drinking root beer and there is no root beer in the house. A child refers to a previous owner by name even though this child was never told the previous owner's name or anything about the former owner.

A MESSAGE FROM THE OTHER SIDE?: My mother crossed over in December 2007. Gene and I had the task of going through all of her things, cleaning and making repairs, etc. I brought home some items from her kitchen that included her bread making machine. It wasn't long after that that when I was sitting at our computer I began to smell the delicious aroma of fresh bread baking. I could smell it throughout the house but it was strongest in the kitchen. I opened the oven door but it wasn't coming from there. And, after opening all the cabinet doors I still wasn't able to determine where it was emanating from. I just gave up and went back to the computer thinking maybe I was just imagining things. It wasn't long that Gene came back from town and when he came in the front door I asked him, "Do you smell that?" Then he replied with, "Smells like bread baking." So it wasn't my imagination! He could smell it too.

This phenomenon occurred one more time after that but the aroma wasn't as strong and it didn't last as long. It has never happened since. Perhaps it was a message from my mother letting us know everything is alright?

MYSTERIOUS FOOTSTEPS: The old Lancaster Cemetery was one helluva cemetery to find! This was our third or fourth attempt over numerous years. On one of the previous tries my cousin went with us. He decided he was going to carry me across Mill Creek. He backed up to me and picked me up piggy-back style. He wasn't much larger than I was and it was very quickly evident that I was too heavy for him. He lost his balance and .... I think you can figure out the rest.

On our last attempt to find the cemetery Gene and I had to take our four-wheel drive pick-up truck past the barn, through the cow pasture, then down a very narrow, rough, dirt road through the woods. Through another cow pasture, then park it and go the rest of the way on foot. Climb over a barbed wire fence, through the weeds, down the creek bank and wade the cold water of Mill Creek. Then through the brush and up the hill.

In the woods Gene and I got separated from each other. He was walking in a westerly direction and I was walking east. I could hear my footsteps in the dry leaves. Then I noticed I could also hear footsteps some distance behind me. When I would stop the other footsteps would stop. When I would turn around and look there was nothing/no-one there.

When I would start walking again so would the other footsteps. After three or four times of hearing these steps and turning around and seeing nothing there I began to get a bit unnerved. Decided I would head back towards Gene which meant I had to walk back in the direction from which I had come and heard the mysterious footsteps. Never saw anything except when I got about half to 3/4 of the way back to where I had started I found a pile of fresh deer poop. The only reasonable explanation I can offer for the footsteps is that perhaps a deer had been following me and when I would turn around and look he was standing still and blending in with the surroundings so much that I didn't see him. But I never heard or saw a deer bound off or any footsteps walking away from me. The only footsteps I heard on the way back were mine. After having tramped around for what seemed like hours and finding only a pile of deer poop Gene and I were walking several hundred yards apart and without each others knowledge gave up at about the same time and started heading for the creek when Gene found the cemetery and gave a holler and I joined him. The cemetery is on a small embankment of Mill Creek. We had been told it was on the top of the hill. No wonder we couldn't find it!! By this time we were about to drop from exhaustion but we got the information and pictures we wanted. Then we had to re-trace our path back to the truck, take the truck back up through the woods to the farmhouse of a relative and collapse on the couch.

Summer 2010: Gene and I tried to visit the cemetery again. Due to health problems Gene didn't climb up the creek embankment so stayed down by the water. I climbed up the embankment and began walking around looking for the cemetery. I immediately noticed footsteps in the leaves behind me just like before. Turned around and looked - nothing there. I mumbled out loud to myself, "Oh, no. Not again." Then I began walking again but there were no more footsteps. I walked around for maybe 30 minutes and never heard anymore footsteps except my own. It was as if whoever/whatever was following me heard my mumbling, realized that they were freaking me out and stopped.

WHO THREW THE BABY FROM THE TRAIN? On 14 August, 1902, in Washington County, Missouri an old farmer, William Helms, was near the Iron Mountain railroad trestle over Big River outside of Irondale. A few minutes after a train had gone by he heard some odd sounds so he investigated and found an old fashioned valise with a baby in it. He determined that the baby had been tossed off the train since it had numerous injuries. Authorities did an investigation but the person who had thrown him from the train was never located.

The Helms family later legally adopted the baby. He was named William Moses Gould Helms - William for his rescuer, Moses for

being found by the river, Gould for the owner of the railroad and Helms for his adopted parents. The Iron Mountain Baby eventually married and had a family of his own and moved to the state of Texas. He died at age 51, was brought back to Washington County (by train) and buried in Hopewell Cemetery.

MAN SHOOTS GHOST: This story was published in the Independent news paper in

1878: "It has given rise to much talk on the subject and every haunted house and dismal byway in the county has had its horrible sights and spiritual apparitions portrayed and repeated by those most suspicious of such characters in our community, and the beast that had never been seen till the old man who related his experience to us discovered it, has since been found dozens of times. One house, more particular than others, situated a short

©-ZIOCK63664

distance from town, has been suspected of being frequented by these unearthly beings and for several nights recently, the evidences of falling rocks on the roof and window lights being broken at the dead hours of night has convinced its inmates, and confirmed the belief generally that the spirit of the old man who committed the 'atrocious crime of incident', within its walls two years ago is yet around. The belief that old man Kasika's spirit was still a frequenter of that section from when his own hand had freed it had been repeated around Mr. John O'Hanlon's fireside from time to time till the younger members of the family, with thorough Stephen Campbell, a nephew, were believers themselves, and now comes the part of a "joke that was not a joke". Last Saturday night one of the younger O'Hanlon boys with Campbell shouldered a shotgun as a protector and started to a neighbor's house on an errand, intending to return, as they did, about eleven o'clock. Mrs. O'Hanlon, without thinking of the gun, and what was to follow, prepared herself in a ghostly robe, and with her little two year old girl, took a position in the yard, and the first thing that met their eyes was the large white object behind the lumber. A demand was made by Campbell, who held the gun, to know who was there. No answer came, save the motion of the wing like hand from the sheet, when in an instant the gun was fired and Mrs. O'Hanlon and her little girl both fell to the ground. They boys were horrified at what they had done, and no time was lost in coming to town for a doctor. Almost twenty shot took effect in Mrs. O'Hanlon's face and two struck the baby...one in the cheek and one in the temple. As the shot were very small the doctor thinks the wound not dangerous, but evidentially had they been larger, both would have been killed. Mrs. O'Hanlon blames herself and not the boys for the foolish act."

MYSTERIOUS MARTINS: The first record of my great, great grandfather, Daniel Martin, in Washington County, Missouri, is in 1865 when he married Narcisses Huitt. But where did he come from and who was he really?

There are two family legends about Daniel. The first is that he killed a man over some woman, changed his last name to Martin and came to Missouri bringing one brother with him. The second legend is that during the Civil War Daniel deserted the Union army after being forced to fight some of his own brothers who were with the Confederacy. Daniel then joined the Confederate army and rode with Quantrill's Raiders for a brief time. At the writing of this book neither legend has been proven or disproven. In the 1890 veterans census Daniel claims to have served four years with Co. G, 48th Virginia Infantry which

Daniel Martin & Jane Hawkins

was a Confederate unit. And there was a Daniel Martin in this unit but documents prove that it isn't my Daniel.

Even though Daniel died in 1915 there is no death certificate for him. His tombstone says he was born in 1842 but doesn't say where. Census records state conflicting information about Daniel's birthplace. One census says Missouri, another Tennessee. Two more census records say Virginia and West Virginia. Death certificates on his children are just as diverse when it comes to saying where their father was born.

Daniel's wife, Narcisses, died in child birth in 1878. Now here is where it becomes confusing. In 1882 Daniel Martin marries Mrs. Jane Hawkins Dicus the former wife of Brad Dicus. I am descended from Daniel Martin and his first wife Narcisses. I am also descended from Jane Hawkins Dicus and her first husband Brad. Both couples are my great, great grandparents. After Daniel's first wife Narcisses died and Jane's first husband Brad ran off and left her, Daniel and Jane eventually married which made my great grandparents, James Martin and Margie Dicus step-brother and sister. And Daniel and Jane had another family. So it was his children, her children and their children.

And here we have another legend that states that Jane was part Indian. I have been told this by several family members. But no one has any proof or knows what tribe. And a DNA test wouldn't be conclusive because if I didn't inherit the Indian genes it wouldn't show up on a test but I could still be part Indian. At least that is what I was told by Ancestry.

Daniel Martin was residing with his son Otis in a log cabin near Courtois Creek in Washington County. One time while carrying in firewood, Daniel tripped and fell on the front porch, seriously injuring himself. George Breakfield sat up with Daniel that night. At around midnight Daniel asked, "What time is it?" When they told him he replied, "Well, maybe I'll make it till morning then." Those were the last words he ever said. He died 28 Feb. 1915. He is buried in Shoal Creek Cemetery, Huzzah, Crawford County.

There is some evidence that Daniel Martin might be related to the Dabney Martin family here in Washington County. But so far there is nothing conclusive. And there is evidence that the Dabney Martin family might be descendants of the Salem witch Susannah North Martin who was one of 14 women executed for witchcraft in Salem, Massachusetts. She was hanged 19 July 1692.

UFO: Gene and I experienced something unusual back in the 90s. One night this light came over our house moving toward the south west. It looked like an extra large star low in the sky. When we would look at it with binoculars you could see multicolored lights inside the white light. We watched it for a good 20 minutes. There was no sound. When it got over the mountain across the valley it went back and forth a few times and up and down a few times then slowly descended and disappeared behind the mountain. Don't know what it was but it didn't act like any kind of aircraft that we knew of.

UFO: One day in 2016 Gene and I were on our way to Potosi when I noticed what appeared to be a silver oblong object in the sky. It didn't look like any kind of plane and there was no contrail. I pointed it out to Gene but before he saw the object it just vanished.

MYSTERIOUS STONES: On the far end of my property there are some stones that look like they outline three sides of a grave. And there is a depression inside of the stones as if a grave has caved in. However, underneath a thin layer of leaves and soil there is what appears to be solid bedrock. This area is part of an old tiff diggins'. It is unknown who put the rocks there and why. Another history mystery.

THE PALMER GHOST: The Palmer ghost is said to be the ghost of a woman who died in the mid 1800s.

FEATHER DEATH CROWNS: Back in the 1980's I went to visit an older cousin, Ollie Breakfield Laramore, who lived in Courtois to interview her about our family tree. During this visit she showed me something that was very unusual. At least it was to me. She opened a small box and inside were two thick circles of clustered feathers. She asked me if I knew what it was or had ever seen anything like that before which I hadn't. Then she told me that when someone dies with their head on a feather pillow the feathers form a circle where the dead person's head was. Well that just creeped me out! I had never heard of this phenomenon before. Since I was mostly interested in the family tree at that time I didn't ask any further about it. Since then numerous people have sent me pictures of the death crowns of family members.

OUIJA BOARD: Pearl Pollard Curran a once famous author is best known for her co-authorship with Patience Worth. Patience was a 17th century spirit that dictated to Pearl Curran by channeling through a Ouija board. In the early 1900's they wrote several best selling novels, short stories, and hundreds of poems. Circa 1898 Pearl's family moved from

St. Louis to Palmer, Washington County, Missouri. Her father worked as a bookkeeper for a lead mining company. The family rented a house in the area and lived between the Alice and Hooker Blount family and the Mary and William League family. Other nearby neighbors were: Benjamin and Myrtle Maxwell, William and Ada Jarvis, Mary Jinkerson, Edward and Anna Wilkinson, Thomas and Martha Skaggs, James and Martha Jenkerson, Stephen and Eliza Conway, and John Mallow.

Pearl eventually took up residence in Chicago, Illinois where she studied voice and music but would come home to visit her family in Missouri. She gave several recitals at the Potosi Opera House, built in 1848, that is now the Masonic Lodge on Breton Street in Potosi.

CROP CIRCLE: Another strange occurrence happened in 1990 near Belgrade. A small mysterious crop circle was discovered in a farmer's field.

BIGFOOT SIGHTING: A few decades ago in Washington County a child found a smelly Bigfoot in a corn crib and ran away in terror.

WHAT WAS IT?: An acquaintance of mine told me some years ago that she and a friend or relative were going home late at night. While almost to Mineral Point they saw something large cross the road in front of their car and it was NOT a bear. They think it was a Bigfoot.

BLOODY PIG: One time back in the 1980s a woman reported that something big came out of the woods and killed one of her pigs and carried it back into the forest. I was told that a deputy went to investigate and found blood all over the place but didn't follow the trail into the woods. Many people thought it was a Bigfoot.

ANOTHER BIGFOOT SIGHTING: A Bigfoot was sighted near Sullivan in Washington

County.   There have been over 100 Bigfoot sightings reported in Missouri.

NIGHT FRIGHT: Well, I read a bunch of spooky stuff at night and then went to bed. I hadn't been in bed long when I felt like I should open my eyes. I thought I saw something white over by the edge of the bed. Nah, must be dreaming. I closed my eyes for a few seconds and then opened them again. OMG - I could see it even clearer now. There was definitely something white there. I fumbled around trying to turn the lamp on not knowing what I might see. Finally got the lamp turned on and looked over.................. It was my cat Dillon sitting there. I was seeing his white throat, chest and abdomen. The rest of him is black so it didn't show up in the dark. Whew!!!! Don't think I should read anymore spooky stuff right before bedtime.

SPOOKY FRONT DOOR: We had just gotten back from a ghost hunt and I transferred the pictures I had taken to my computer and was looking for any unusual anomalies.   Since it was summer I had the front door open but the screen door was closed.

I was really concentrating on my work when I heard the front door creaking. It really sounded spooky. I could see the front door from the computer room so I just automatically looked to see what was making the noise. Then I saw that the front door was slowly closing on its own!! As the adrenalin rushed through me my first thought was that *something* had come home with us. I just kind of froze for a few seconds as I watched the front door closing. When I finally got up and went over to the door and looked behind it there was my cat Tommy with his front paws on the door pushing it shut. I breathed a big sigh of relief as I told him, "Don't do that after mommy has just gotten home from a ghost hunt!!!"

PSYCHIC: I was told by several people that my great grandmother, Margie Dicus Martin, was psychic and that she got it from her mother, Jane Hawkins Dicus Martin, who was supposedly part American Indian. Margie could also read tea leaves in the bottom of a tea cup. They said that many of her predictions came true.

A cousin of mine, M. C. B., was also psychic. She could hold a picture of someone that she did not know and had never met and tell you what kind of person they are. She did this with the picture of a relative that I knew but she didn't. She held the picture in one hand and laid her other hand gently on the picture. After a minute or so she began to tell me all about this person and she was correct on everything.

My cousin, who was a retired nurse who had been married to a doctor, also told me about a phenomenon that sometimes happened to people when they died. She referred to it as "The Spark Of Life". When the person died a small spark would exit their mouth at the time of their death. She added that she and her doctor husband had seen this many times.

GATE TO HELL: There is a mine in Washington County that is considered to be the world's deepest mineral mine. It's been said that it is a gateway to Hell with screams of the damned emanating from the shaft.

HAUNTED STAGE COACH HOUSE: It is said that the old "Stagecoach" house on Missouri Street was haunted. This house no longer exists.

PREMONITIONS: I have been somewhat psychic my whole life. When I was younger I used to get premonitions more frequently. Now that I'm older I don't get them as frequently but I still get them occasionally. Unfortunately I can't control them, they just come and go on their own.

Usually they are a really strong sense that something bad is going to happen but one time I actually had a vision. I was at the firehouse where Gene worked. He had the hood up on our truck to fix something wrong in the motor. I was sitting in the driver's seat.

Suddenly I had a vision of him getting electrocuted. The vision flashed in front of me like an old time silent movie. About a minute later Gene quickly pulled his arm out of the motor of the truck hollering, "ouch!" He had gotten shocked while touching the battery.

Another time I had a dream that came true. I was in bed sick and Gene was fixing me something to eat. I dreamt of a nice delicious hamburger, cut in half, and laying on a plate. When he brought my food in to me it was a hamburger cut in half and laying on a plate! Now some people might say that I smelled the hamburger cooking while I was sleeping. But, what about it being cut in half? There is no way I could have known that. He had never cut any hamburger in half before or since.

Now, if my premonitions could just give me some winning lottery numbers.................

JEFFERSON COUNTY

LOST HISTORY MUSEUM: The Lost History Museum is located in the town of Valles Mines,

©-ZIOCK63664

founded by Francois Valle when he built a log cabin there circa 1749. The cabin has been added to over the years and is now part of The Lost History Museum which has a reputation for being haunted.

Gene and I participated in a paranormal

investigation there with Just Curious Paranormal in 2011. During the investigation the following incidents happened: A flashlight turned on and off by itself without anyone touching it. I detected a cold spot with my laser thermometer in one corner of the office and a K2 meter in the office responded twice indicating a ghost was present.

In an upstairs room one of the investigators sitting in an arm chair said she could feel the chair vibrating. A voice recorder picked up some very faint whispers. Orbs were photographed on both the first and second floors. Several popping sounds were heard through out the evening however it is unsure if this was paranormal or the house settling as the temperature outside dropped. At the end of the investigation I found that my voice recorder that had been left downstairs had been turned off while everyone was upstairs.

DEMAREE HOUSE: Cornelius Demaree settled in House Springs circa 1837. He was a merchant, operated a store and was also the

Endangered Old Home in House Springs, Mo.
ZIOCK63664 - 5 May 2015

first postmaster in the area. I was able to get this home on Missouri Preservation's list of Endangered Homes. I've been told that the home is haunted and that someone actually photographed the ghost.

HAUNTED CEMETERY: Kimmswick is a small river town on the Mississippi River. It was founded in 1859 by merchant Theodore Kimm who had come to Jefferson County from St. Louis. The Kimm family cemetery is reported to be haunted.

THE BATTLE OF BLACKWELL: The Battle of Blackwell during the Civil War was actually two battles that took place about two miles apart. The first one was at the railroad bridge over Big River in Jefferson County and the second one was at the village of Blackwell in St. Francois County.

The railroad bridge was being guarded by approximately 45 Union soldiers. At dawn on 15 October 1861 the area was attacked by 400 Confederate soldiers under command of Gen. Jeff "Swamp Fox" Thompson. The Yankees awoke to the sound of gunfire and emerged from their tents with bullets whistling around them. The rebels quickly captured the Union soldiers but did them no harm. One

Union officer, however, refused to relinquish his sword. Gen. Thompson was summoned but the officer still refused. Thompson then called up his Indian orderly named Ajax. Ajax dismounted and started for the officer with his tomahawk and the officer, upon threat of being murdered and scalped, ran to Thompson begging to turn over his sword.

The bridge was then burned and the prisoners were released upon taking the oath not to serve during the war unless exchanged. This was the only Civil War battle fought in Jefferson County.

ST. FRANCOIS COUNTY

THE BATTLE OF BLACKWELL: The second battle was at the town of Blackwell in St. Francois County. About 50 men of the 33rd Illinois under Capt. Lippincott were stationed there. It was reported that both battles resulted in seven killed and 22 wounded.

In 2016 we went with some paranormal friends from Souls Paranormal Research on a daytime investigation at the location where the second Battle of Blackwell took place. Now it is a beautiful, peaceful area on the bank of the Big River and it is hard to believe any kind of violence ever took place there.

I did, however, get some activity with my witching rods. There have been previous investigations there at night time where there was quite a bit of paranormal activity. I would like to go back again at night as that is when most of the spooky stuff happens.

HAUNTED BLACKWELL: Blackwell's Station,

now referred to as just Blackwell, is a small

town in northern St. Francois County, Missouri. It is on the west bank of Big River on the historic St. Louis and Iron Mountain railroad which was constructed in 1858. The town was named in honor of Jeremiah Blackwell, a slave holder and soldier from the War of 1812, who settled in the area during the 1820's.

As one approaches Blackwell you will descend lower and lower to the river valley. It is basically a ghost town now. Some buildings are gone completely while others lay in collapsed ruins.

Blackwell is said to be one of the scariest places in Missouri with some people saying that the whole area is evil and that Satanism is practiced in certain locations.

Legends of the town of Blackwell and surrounding area being haunted are numerous. Many people swear they have been chased by a phantom car. Others claim to have seen a faceless flying nun, a ghost couple and a ghost train. Others state that they have seen shadows jumping from tree to tree, and unexplainable sounds, orbs and other weird occurrences. There are rumors of an Indian curse and it has been reported that one can stand on the Big River Bridge and hear the sound of Indian drums emanating from the river valley. Another legend tells of Judge Blackwell who liked to hang people from the (old) Blackwell Bridge.

Another odd thing about Blackwell is the number of deaths on the railroad tracks either at or near Blackwell. 18 deaths and there may be more that there is no longer any record of. Some fell from trains, some were sleeping by the tracks using the ties for a pillow, but most were walking the tracks.

IS HE DEAD??? "While discussing the Youngers and the Jameses, it is just as well to

Sam's grave Hampton Cemetery, Elvins, Mo. The day we visited this was the only grave that had flowers on it.

remember that they were not the only dangerous men in the dug out. There were others along in the [18]'60's. Missouri woods were full of men who could hit a bulls eye or a human target ten times out of ten. Only of few of them, however, kept on shooting long enough after the [Civil] war to ensure lasting reputations." *Butler Missouri Times*

Sam Hildebrand was southeast Missouri's notorious outlaw. In the Confederate Army he became a soldier/guerilla who was greatly feared. He began a reign of killings and terror that continued throughout and after the war until Sam's alleged death in 1872. He killed many people with his rifle, which he had named "Kill Devil." For every person that he killed he carved a notch in the rifle stock.

Sam was supposedly killed in Pinkneyville, Illinois, in 1872. His body was positively identified by two St. Louis policemen, one of whom had grown up with Sam. Sam's body was shipped back to Farmington, St. Francois County, and he was buried in the Hampton Cemetery.

In 1877 a newspaper published an article about a man claiming to be Hildebrand stopping to visit with an old farmer in Madison County, Missouri. The farmer had been a neighbor of Sam for three years. The farmer, who was said to be an honorable citizen, eventually recognized Sam and Sam spent the night. The next day Sam continued on to Illinois.

Another Sam sighting took place on 18 June, 1905, in Vernon, Texas. It was said that he was at a store near the crossing of the Red River. He was recognized but disappeared before the law could be notified. In 1905 a Bonne Terre, Missouri, newspaper published an article stating that Sam had been living on a farm near Lawton, Oklahoma. His identity was clearly established, a warrant was sworn out for his arrest but before it could be served he disappeared.

The following article concerning Sam Hildebrand was published in July, 1905:

> The St. Louis papers are devoting a good deal of space as to whether Sam Hilderbrand (sic) is dead or not and as to whether he is buried in St. Francois County. Mr. George Helderbrand, formerly sheriff of Madison county, has this to say in regard to the same: "Sam Helderbrand (sic) was not killed in Illinois, as reported years ago, and his body is not buried in St. Francois county, Mo." "Old Man Boyer and Billy Townsend of Madison county, were

intimate friends of his cousin Sam and that about fifteen years ago Billy Townsend moved to Arkansas, and after he had been there a few years Old Man Boyer received a letter from him saying "Our old friend Preacher Morgan (the name by which Sam was known to his intimate friends) spent the night with me. He is in good health and on his way to Texas."

Continuing, Mr. Helderbrand said: "The body buried in St. Francois county was never identified as that of Sam Helderbrand. His son who was called to St. Francois county to identify the body, could not do it. He said it looked like his father in some respects, and in others it did not, and that was as far as the identification went."

"If Sam Helderbrand (sic) is dead," said George, "he has died in the last twelve months, and I don't think he is dead."

I guess no one will ever know for sure. Another history mystery.

OUCH!: 2005 or 2006. This is one incident I

could've done without. When we were leaving the Hampton Cemetery after photographing Sam Hildebrand's tombstone there were about three or four concrete steps to go down to get to the concrete sidewalk and then the street. When I was on the second step I tripped and fell down onto the sidewalk bypassing the other steps completely. My head just barely missed the bumper of our truck. When I hit the sidewalk it knocked my glasses off of my face, scraped my hands and took some skin off of my knees in the same spot that I skinned them in our motorcycle wreck back in 1974. People later were teasing me that Sam Hildebrand pushed me down the steps. But it has been said that Sam never hurt a woman so don't think it was him.

FRANKLIN COUNTY

THE UNION SCREAMING HOUSE: The town of Union in Franklin County is the location of the Union Screaming House which is now considered one of the most haunted and violent houses in America. It is inhabited by demons and many people have been chased from the house, screaming in panic and terror.

The Catholic Church wrote a lengthy report about the supernatural activities at the house which included physical harm, sexual assault and even caused two persons to be institutionalized. The home was featured on a Discovery Channel series, "A Haunting," and a third season episode titled "Fear House."

Best selling author Steven LaChance has written several books about his horrifying experiences when he lived in the house. He consulted paranormal investigators, psychics and priests but the nightmare continued until he and his three children were finally driven from the home after three years of residence there.

SOMETHING'S DEAD IN THE CEMETERY: I don't remember the name of the cemetery anymore or it's exact location only that it was next to a roadway. The whole time I was there looking at tombstones I kept smelling something dead. I assumed it was an animal that had gotten hit by a car. I finally got curious and started looking for it. I followed the smell to where it was the strongest but never found any dead animal. I finally decided to just leave as it was very uncomfortable smelling something dead – especially in a cemetery.

CROW CEMETERY: We went with the Franklin County Paranormal Society on this investigation. The weather was pleasant with a full moon and a few clouds, temperature in the 70's.

This is a pre-1930s cemetery with over 660 burials. We arrived at the cemetery at approximately 8:30 p.m., and began organizing our equipment.

The batteries in my cousin's camera went dead. After replacing her camera batteries we headed into the cemetery. My cousin photographed an orb atop the tombstone of James Crow. Another investigator photographed a small burst of light above a tombstone in about the middle of the cemetery. Part way through the investigation my cousin and I took a break and went down by the vehicles. Upon returning to the cemetery my cousin felt a cool spot near the cemetery gate. As we both proceeded through the gate into the cemetery we noticed an immediate temperature drop as if the entire cemetery was cooler than on the outside of the graveyard.

Later, while participating in an EVP pow wow, I was sitting near and facing the tombstone of Martha Philips when I observed a small (approximately five inch square) shadow move across the middle of the stone to the right and disappear into the darkness of night. My cousin was sitting on my left and two other investigators were on my left behind my cousin. They tried making shadows on the stone to see if it had been any of us who possibly inadvertently made the shadow and determined it was not any of us.

After the pow wow two of the investigators left shortly before myself and my cousin. As we began to leave I heard an unusual squeaking type of sound at the edge of the cemetery by the woods but my cousin did not hear it. As we got almost to the cemetery gate my cousin turned to say something to me and she briefly observed the appearance of a small girl dressed in a flowing white gown like a christening dress. It only lasted 2 or 3 seconds moving from one tombstone to another over towards the woods. We shined our flashlights over in that area but saw nothing.

Everyone left the cemetery at around 10:30 p.m. Gene and I came back to Washington County while the others of the team proceeded to another location.

THE LEGEND OF MERAMEC CAVERNS:
Meramec Caverns is a four and a half mile long cave located near Stanton in the Ozark Mountains of Franklin County. It is a four star rated tourist attraction and is the most visited cave in Missouri.

American Indians used the cave as shelter in prehistoric times. And, it was the first cave west of the Mississippi River to be explored by Europeans in the early 1700s.

The cave claims to have been the hideout of Missouri's infamous outlaw Jesse James.

Some of my husband's relatives claim that the Carrolls are related to Jesse James by way of Margaret Carroll who was married to James M. James a supposed cousin of Jesse. Margaret Carroll was my husband's great aunt. Also Jesse James' great grandmother was Mary Hines and Gene Carroll's great, great, great grandmother was Margaret Elizabeth Hines.

Frank James visited Margaret Carroll and her husband, James, often. One time when Frank and Jesse spent a week with Margaret Carroll James there was a big bank robbery - Jesse James strikes again! After that Margaret swore Jesse didn't do half he was credited with.

Below is my story of Jesse James and the Gads Hill train robbery in reference to Meramec Caverns:

Jesse James and his brother Frank (sons of a Baptist minister) were well known Missouri outlaws. Their life of crime began at an early age when they joined the notorious Confederate Civil War guerilla band of William Clarke Quantrill which terrorized the Kansas-Missouri border zone. After the war the James brothers continued robbing banks, trains, and stages from 1866 to 1881 with more than twenty-five raids in and around Missouri amounting to a take of about a half a million dollars.

Missouri produced many outlaws after the Civil War but it is basically the James gang that is credited for Missouri being nicknamed "The Outlaw State". Some people thought of Jesse as a sort of Robin Hood who robbed the rich and gave to the poor. Others described him as a lawless, merciless, murdering robber who terrorized the countryside from Missouri to Texas. Rewards of up to $5,000.00 were offered for Jesse and his gang - DEAD OR ALIVE. Pursuers were warned to take no chances and to shoot to kill as these were the most desperate men in America.

Strong evidence indicates that the "James Gang" committed the first Missouri train robbery which took place on the Iron

Mountain Railroad at a small, remote flag station called Gads Hill in Wayne County (approximately an hour south of Washington County) on Saturday, 31 January, 1874. The robbers held the citizens of the tiny town prisoner while waiting for the little Rock Express which would be coming from St. Louis. A red flag was put out to assure that the train would stop. When the train arrived at Gads Hill at 4:45 p.m. the unsuspecting conductor stepped off to greet his new passengers but instead had a six-shooter stuck in his face and was told, "..........stand still or I'll blow the top of your head off!"

The train was then boldly robbed by five large masked men (over six feet tall) heavily armed with navy revolvers and double barreled shotguns. The passengers were threatened and told to "shell out" or have their "brains blown out." They were then robbed of their cash, watches and jewelry. A man suspected of being a Pinkerton detective was taken to another part of the train and striped naked. As the robbers were carrying money, mail and packages from the train Mr. Wilson the express agent commented to one of them, "I have always been in the habit of having people sign a receipt when I deliver them packages." The outlaw replied, "O, well, just hand me your book and I'll sign." He took the book and wrote in the back, "ROBBED"!

The robbery lasted about 40 minutes. When the robbers were through they shook hands with the engineer and then galloped away into the woods with over $4,000.00 worth of loot. It was suspected that the gang consisted of Jesse and Frank James, Arthur McCoy, and Cole and Bud Younger. The incident created".......a hell of an excitement in this part of the country!"

The next day a posse of approximately twenty-five men was organized and left in pursuit of the outlaws. One version of the story states that they went in a northwest direction through Texas and Wright counties and toward Laclede County. However, according to the legend of Meramec Caverns which is in Franklin County near the Washington County line, the James Gang was tracked to the Caverns (at that time called Saltpeter Cave).

The posse waited outside the entrance of the cave for three days. When the outlaws didn't come out the posse went in, but all they found were horses wandering around in the dark. The outlaws had managed to escape from the cave by a secret route and were not apprehended. Another history mystery.

ST. LOUIS CITY:

St. Louis is one of the most haunted cities in the United States. The earliest settlements in what would later become St. Louis were built by the Indians who lived in the area from about 600-1300 A.D. Their numerous mounds date back to circa 1050 however Sugarloaf Mound is the only one that survives today.

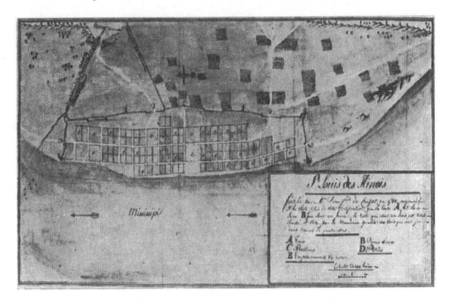

St. Louis was established as a fur trading post on the west bank of the Mississippi River in 1764 by Pierre Laclede and Auguste Chouteau.

The city was fortified on it's north, west, and southern sides with a wall which had towers and gates. On a 1780s map of the city it shows three main streets: Rue Des Granges, Rue De L'Eglise, and Grand Rue.

The city rapidly expanded from its original 30 settlers to a population of 1,000 in 1804. In 1811 St. Louis only covered an area of 7.63 square miles and had a population of about 1,200 with most of them being in the Laclede's Landing area.

As the city continued to grow an unusual discovery was made, in 1816, of large human footprints imbedded in a limestone slab. They had not been carved out but had been made by the pressure of standing in the soft stone. The stone hardened about 250 million years ago. Who made them? Another history mystery.

St. Louis now has an estimated population of over 315,000 and is the largest metropolitan area in Missouri. It has survived many disasters of epidemics, fire, wars, earthquakes, tornadoes, politics, crime, etc., and is home to beautiful old structures and many, ancient spirits.

GHOST STORIES: In 2015 my husband was in the Des Peres Hospital in St. Louis County to have a pacemaker installed after a heart attack earlier in the year. I wanted to stay with him but there was no place for me to sleep that night so I called my cousin Paul who lived about 20 minutes away in St. Louis and he came and got me and I spent the night with Paul and Dolores. We sat up till midnight telling scary ghost stories.........then slept with the lights on.

LEMP MANSION: Built in 1868 it is considered the most haunted building in the city of St. Louis and one of the ten most haunted places in America. The Lemp family members all died under tragic circumstances in this home including several suicides.

My great grandfather, August Ziock Sr., worked for a few years at the Lemp Brewery as a book keeper.

One time Gene and I had dinner at the Lemp Mansion with a Civil War Re-enactors group. Didn't experience anything paranormal at that time. Maybe the party was too loud and boisterous and scared all the ghosts away.

MISSING ANCESTOR: Richard "Dick" Horrocks, my great uncle, was born 1894 in St. Louis, Missouri. He appears in the 1920 census of that city but then disappears. I was told when I was younger that he was a gangster during prohibition and was killed in a gang fight. However I could never find a death

certificate or any other evidence of his demise. When I asked my aunt Lilian Ziock Palmer about him all she would say is that he was a gangster and just disappeared.

Looking for him would be like searching for a needle in a hay stack. However a friend of a friend found him alive and well living in a suburb of Boston in 1942!! It was his WWII draft registration card that provided this information. So I began a new search but could find nothing on him between 1920 and 1942. After 1942 he disappears again and search after search has produced no new clues. Another history mystery.

THE DEVIL MADE HIM DO IT: When I was a member of a paranormal group I helped with historical research for the movie "The Haunted Boy" although I am not listed in the credits. I found on the internet where the young man that this movie is about was living out on or near the east coast.

He is the one that the movie "The Exorcist" was based on. He lived on the fifth floor of St. Vincent's Asylum and it has been said that he used to ride on top of the elevator car as it went up and down it's shaft and he would yell and scream obscenities as loudly as he could.

St. Vincent's has been remodeled into modern apartments and is now known as Castle Park Apartments. Several locations in the building are haunted. It is listed on the National Register of Historic Places.

NEW PICKERS CEMETERY: One time at the New Pickers cemetery (the cemetery is now renamed Gatewood Gardens) office in St. Louis the management told me a couple of stories about their cemetery. They said for awhile a man would come to the cemetery every day and sit beside his wife's grave and play the harmonica for exactly one hour then he would leave.

In another incident they said when they came to the office one morning there was a man sitting on the front steps holding a shovel. He wanted to know where his mother's grave was. Said she had been buried here too long and he wanted to dig her up, take her home and bury her in the back yard where she belonged.

MIDNIGHT MUSIC: One time when my parents lived on Exeter Ave. in Shrewsbury, St. Louis they had an over night guest. I think it was one of my mother's sisters. She was sleeping in the living room. Also in the living was a piano. My parents neglected to tell her that we had a black named Midnight. And this cat liked to walk on the piano keys. So in the middle of the night Midnight began walking on the keyboard and since it was dark my aunt couldn't see the black cat. When mom came into the room to tell her sister to not be afraid it was too late. When mom turned the light on in the room there was her terrified sister sitting up with eyes as big as saucers staring at that piano.

ST. LOUIS COUNTY

INDIAN MOUNDS: Ancient Indian tribes used to be very prevalent in the area especially near the Missouri River. I found two stone artifacts on my parents property. After I got married and moved further up the road I lived close to two Indian mounds. My neighbor, a farmer, whose property one of the mounds was on gave me permission to hunt artifacts in his field after he was finished plowing. I have many stone artifacts that appear to be mostly from the Archaic period (3,000 B.C.) As with the city of St. Louis there is the possibility of many ancient spirits in the county as well.

STRANGE LIGHTS IN CEMETERY AT NIGHT: When I was a teenager my cousin,

Billie Jean Martin, lived with my parents and I for a couple of years. She and I would ride our horses to the back of Babler State Park where we could access the trail that led to the riding stables. We would pack a lunch in the saddle bags and while the horses were resting at the stable we would go across the street to the old Coleman Family Cemetery in the edge of the woods, sit on the tombstones and eat our lunch.

One day when speaking with the stable manager he told us that sometimes when he was working late in the office he would see strange lights moving around over at the cemetery. To this day I'm still not sure if he was really telling the truth or just trying to scare a couple of kids.

Billie Jean and I had been in the cemetery several times and never experienced anything supernatural. There was only one time we got a little nervous. The wind suddenly picked up and the sky seemed to get slightly darker and along with it I got this overwhelming feeling of fear and dread so we left the cemetery and went back to the stable. I don't think we ever went back to the cemetery after that.

OLD HAUNTED HOME: I have a personal connection to this beautiful antebellum home. I have researched it's history but I cannot reveal all facts without giving away its location. I managed to get this home listed on Missouri Preservation's endangered homes list.

This house is quite a paranormally active place. Numerous apparitions have been encountered in the house and on the road to the house. There have been reports of footsteps being heard along with strange lights. A woman on the front porch wearing a white flowing dress has been seen, a man in a leather trench coat with a hat on was seen walking along the road in the direction of the house and when spoken to he vanished. Another time there was a woman in a white dress and a man wearing a long coat and a top hat carrying lanterns were seen just floating down the road moving away from the house.

In 2005 Gene and I were with a paranormal group on their preliminary walk through of the vacant house. One member set up a video camera to film in one of the downstairs rooms where he had photographed an orb earlier while the rest of us explored the house.

Another member of the group who had never met me and didn't know my name spoke with an elderly female spirit in an upstairs room over the kitchen. When she was telling about the incident later she said that the spirit said the name "Esther" to her. When I informed her that that was my name and that I have a personal connection to the house we both kind of freaked a little bit. By now it was almost time to leave and I didn't want to go back into the house by myself after everyone left.

Everyone finally decided to go to another investigative location except for Gene and I. We old folks were too tired and had a long drive home so we didn't go with them. Later when the video was reviewed that had been filming on the first floor across the hallway from the kitchen there was a ball of mist in the vacant room. It moved across the room maybe eight inches above the floor and then dissipated into the wall.

CEMETERY ADVENTURES

GRAVE WITCHING: In October of 2014 I learned something new - grave witching. I've heard about it, read about it but had never experienced it. Was always kind of skeptical about it. But while taking some Blackwell descendants to a couple of old cemeteries waaaayyyyy back in the woods to visit some of their ancestor's graves I experienced grave witching for the first time.

One of the men in our group had some dowsing/witching rods with him and told me to try them out. It was absolutely amazing! It actually works! I was holding one rod loosely in each hand and when I would walk over a grave the rods would cross - all on their own! And I would feel a kind of magnetic energy in them when this would happen. It was awesome! I told Gene that we need to get some witching rods to add to our cemetery kit so the next day he went out and bought some rods and had Keith at Merx's mechanic shop bend them for him and now I have my witching rods! It is said, however, that this phenomenon does not work for everyone. You have to have "the power" within you and not everybody does. For some people it works and for others it doesn't. Don't know why - that's just the way it is.

HIDDEN TOMBSTONE: After getting permission to visit this cemetery Gene and I had to trek through shoulder high weeds to get to the woods. When we got to the cemetery there was a type of spiked fence around it and the gate was locked with a pad lock. I wasn't able to climb over the fence so I shinnied up a tree that was a few inches from the fence and then dropped down inside the enclosure. I had been asked to photograph the tombstone of Ambrose Powell in the Cresswell-Mathews Cemetery but could not find him anywhere.

After the trouble we had getting to the cemetery and after photographing other tombstones I was getting really tired and had decided to give up trying to find Ambrose and go home. I started walking toward the fence to leave and after a few steps I tripped over something in the thick layer of leaves which covered the cemetery. Wondering what it was that I tripped over I reached down and brushed the leaves back. It was the corner of a fallen tombstone. I brushed away the remaining leaves only to discover it was Ambrose! It was almost as though he had reached up and tripped me so I could find him and get his picture too - the one I most wanted.

I SEE THE LIGHT: The Wallen Cemetery was kind of hard to find. We drove around and drove around. Stopped at about six different places to ask directions but no one knew. We knew we had to be in the right area when we were on Doc Wallen Road. Anyway, we finally came across an old farmer on his tractor and he knew right where it was. We had driven past it once but didn't see it as it is barely visible from the road. So we finally made it to the cemetery and none too soon as we had a flat tire. So we pulled up into the cow pasture (where the cemetery is) and while I photographed tombstones Gene changed the flat tire.

I noticed something unusual while photographing. When I would aim my camera at a tombstone the sun would come out from behind a cloud and I would get a very nice bright picture of the stone then the sun went behind a cloud again. When I aimed my camera at another tombstone the sun would come back from behind a cloud again as if it were deliberately shining a light on the tombstone. I didn't count how many times this happened but it was maybe 10 or more times. Coincidence??????

LOST: In August, 2002 we went out on a picture taking expedition. Tried to find the Shoal Creek Church and Cemetery in Crawford County, Missouri. I've been there before but it was a loooooooooooong time ago. Anyway, I told Gene, "I think we're supposed to turn here." So he turned. Weeeeeeeeell......we drove around and drove around for maybe 45 minutes on gravel roads that all started looking alike. Finally we turned onto another road and saw tire tracks in the gravel. Gene said, "It looks like someone has been through this way." I replied, "Maybe it was us!" So we drove around and drove around and drove around some more till we finally came out on Hwy. 19 at Cherryville. By this time we were getting hungry so drove up to Steelville to get some lunch. After that we paid a quick visit to the Steelville Cemetery then came home. Never did find the Shoal Creek Church but got a lot of other good pictures along the way.

I DON'T DO MORNINGS: More proof that I don't do mornings well: We got up early and went to a local restaurant for breakfast before meeting some out of state cousins at Caledonia later that morning and showing them the Bellevue Presbyterian Cemetery. Gene parked the truck in the parking lot of the restaurant and I opened the truck door and tried to get out. But I couldn't. Hhhhhhmmm - I wonder why? Then I discovered I had forgotten to unfasten my seat belt. DUH

COWS IN THE CEMETERY: Gene and I go by the Nicholson Cemetery every time on our way to and from Potosi. We left very early one morning as we had business to take care of in St. Louis which is about a two hour drive from where we live. I always tell people that I am not a morning person - never have been, never will be. My brain and body just do not function well in the mornings and this story is a prime example of that.

This was the first time I had been by the cemetery since the cows arrived. In my bleary-eyed, early morning stupor I spotted those two cows - one in each front corner of the cemetery. Right away I exclaimed to Gene, "OMG!! The cows are in the cemetery!!!! We better stop by the Sheriff's Department and let them know so they can contact the Nicholsons to come get them out of the cemetery!!" As we go on down the road Gene just looks at me with this weird look on his face. So I say, "What??!!" He says, "You can't be serious." I replied that I was serious - didn't want the cows messing up the cemetery. Then he proceeds to tell me that the cows are artificial and put there intentionally for decoration. So then I give him a weird look. I really thought he was joking so he turns around and goes back driving v - e - r- y s - l - o - w - l - y past the cemetery. Was I surprised to realize they really were cow statues! DUH! I hate to admit it when he is right but I'm just glad he didn't decide to be really mean and let me make a total fool of myself by taking me to the Sheriff's Department and letting me go in and actually report the cows being in the cemetery.

THE COWS ARE AFTER US!: One time back in the 80s Gene and I went with another couple to visit a cemetery. It was a small cemetery out in the middle of a cow pasture. And the cows were way over at the other side of the pasture.

The men stayed at the gate of the pasture talking to the owner while my friend and I hiked out to the cemetery. It was enclosed by a chain link fence and a bit weedy but we were still able to make out the inscriptions on the tombstones so we began writing them down in tablets that we had brought with us. Well, while we were concentrating on doing that the cows had become curious and were walking over to the cemetery. When we finished copying inscriptions and looked up from our work the cows had gotten considerably closer.

My friend stated, "Oh, no! The cows are coming!" We started walking toward the pasture gate and the cows started following us. When we started running to the gate the cows started trotting along behind us. But we made it out of the pasture safe and sound and the cows just stopped and stood there with confused looks on their faces. But even people sometimes give us confused looks when they see us copying/photographing tombstones. It's something only other genealogists understand.

DOGS IN THE CEMETERIES: Some times when we visit cemeteries dogs from nearby neighbors will come into the cemetery to see what we are doing and watch us. Several times we've had dogs join us.

CATS IN THE CEMETERIES: One time in a cemetery a cat from a nearby house got curious and came into the cemetery to watch us. It followed along with us for awhile then became disinterested and left.

Another time while at the Springer Cemetery it was a warm summer day and we were at a farm so left the windows rolled down without worrying about anyone stealing anything. As we were getting in our car to leave we found a cat in the back seat laying there as if it owned the car and was waiting for it's chauffer. When I opened the back door it calmly got out and went to sit on the back porch of the farm house.

THERE'S A GOAT IN THE CEMETERY!! A very friendly goat was grazing next to the Cub Creek Cemetery. When I finished photographing tombstones and got into the truck to leave he jumped through the fence and wanted to go with us! Fortunately he was tethered to a near by tree so he didn't get very far.

SNAKE IN THE CEMETERY: Back in the 80's I visited the Steelville Cemetery in Crawford County, to look for ancestor tombstones there. I found the row that they were buried in and began copying inscriptions. This was in mid to late summer and the grass was dry and made a crinkling sound when walked on. While I was standing there I heard an odd sound of something coming through the grass. I looked all around but couldn't see anything so moved to the next tombstone. The sound stopped when I moved.

When I stood still to copy the next tombstone inscription I heard the sound again. Looked all around but didn't see anything. Finally I turned to go to another tombstone and that's when I saw it. It was a little snake coming through the dry grass toward me. He knew exactly when I spotted him and raised the front half of his body up in the air. We stood there looking at each other for a minute or two then I told him if he didn't bother me I wouldn't bother him.

I was done with copying tombstone inscriptions so I made a wide circle around him and went back to my car. He stayed still and watched me the entire time. Got in the car and as I drove away I looked in the side mirror and he was still there watching me. Don't know how long it took him to continue on his way.

ANTS IN THE CEMETERY: In May, 1992 Gene and I took a trip to Lafayette, Louisiana and our route went right through Ouachita Parish where some of my Henderson ancestors had resided. Of course we just had to stop at Monroe so I could poke around through the courthouse records for a few hours! We stopped briefly at Bosco to observe some very cute rare dwarf cats before proceeding on to Alexandria. While there we learned there was a Henderson family cemetery near the campground we were staying at. While visiting this cemetery I was bitten on the top of my foot by a fire ant. Now I know how they got their name....it burned like fire! It also left a red, itchy bump on my foot for more than a year.

NO CHICKENS IN THE CEMETERY: Some years ago the Daily Journal newspaper provided a discussion forum online. People were talking about how the old cemetery in Ste. Genevieve is supposed to be haunted. Then someone suggested that on the upcoming Saturday we all meet at midnight at the cemetery and see what happens. Many people agreed including myself. However the closer it got to Saturday more and more people were coming up with excuses why they couldn't be there. By Saturday everyone had chickened out. I still wanted to go but wasn't about to go by myself. So much for our big cemetery ghost hunt! Cluck, cluck!

* * * * * * * * * * * * * * * * * * *

Circa 1954 my parents moved from Shrewsbury, St. Louis, to Chesterfield, St. Louis County. I grew up on Wild Horse Creek Road behind the Antioch Baptist Church Cemetery. I could see tombstones out my bedroom window and would often cut through the cemetery to visit a friend that lived on the other side of the church and parsonage.

HORSE IN THE CEMETERY: It wasn't unusual when I was growing up to have a neighbor call and say "your horse is out." One time the phone rang in the middle of the night and a neighbor said "Your horse just went through my front yard."

One afternoon Gene called me from the fire house (where he worked) which was maybe a quarter mile up the road. It seems a highway patrol officer was driving by the Antioch Church graveyard and Red Cloud was calmly grazing in the cemetery. So the officer drove on up to the firehouse to ask if any of the firemen knew who that horse belonged to that was in the cemetery. Gene walked out into the parking lot and looked down the road. Just as he thought it was Red Cloud. Came back in and told the officer he would call the owner. The police officer drove back down to the cemetery and parked there to keep an eye on Red Cloud till someone came for him. When Gene called, mom and I got the rope halter and went right up to Red Cloud, slipped it over his head and walked him down the driveway to his corral.

Another time someone called and said that he was trying to swim the slough down in Centaur. And he liked to cut through the woods sometimes and go over to the next hill and visit with Lewises mules. Daddy was always fixing fences and that horse would still find ways to get out and go on walk-abouts. I think it was a competition between him and daddy and it makes me think of that song "Don't Fence Me In".

HALLOWEEN: Since my parents and I lived behind a cemetery and our driveway went right past the end of the cemetery at the edge of the woods we never got any trick-or-treaters. No one wanted to walk past the cemetery at night. But every year near Halloween my father would always buy a truck load of candy "just in case". He would occasionally sample the candy before Halloween and when we didn't get any trick-or-treaters then he would gradually eat it all himself.

VOICE IN THE DARK: One day a high school friend came to spend the weekend. When she and I were talking to Bill Sutton who lived across the street he dared us to come up the drive-way and walk the entire length of the edge of the cemetery at midnight. And so he would know that we did it we were to ring the church bell that was in front of the church. This big bell was low to the ground so it could be pushed and it was surrounded by shrubbery except for the front side. And the church had just gotten a new preacher.

Anyway, at around midnight I got a flashlight and my friend and I walked up the drive-way and turned left at the corner of the cemetery. When we got up to the bell we started pushing on it. It was heavy but once we got the momentum going the bell rang out loudly and easily. After a couple of minutes a voice from the other side of the shrubbery said, "Hey, what's the big idea!" Well that scared the dickens out of us and we took off running for home. About half-way back to my driveway I dropped the flashlight. But I was running so fast it took me another five feet or more before I got stopped. My friend was way ahead of me. Now the dilemma here was whether to go back for the flashlight or keep on running. If I went back for the flashlight I might get caught by "the voice in the dark" but if I came home without daddy's favorite flashlight I would catch hell for that. I went back for the flashlight then took off running for home again! When I saw

Bill Sutton a day or two later I told him we had completed his dare (and initiated the new preacher) and asked if he heard us ringing the church bell. His reply, "I wasn't home that night." Gggrrr! And I sure wasn't going to do it again!!!

BOO!: I was never afraid of the cemetery during the day. But one time when my uncle, Bill Martin, was spending the weekend with us he talked me into walking up to the road after dark to get the mail which no one had gotten that day. As I walked up the drive-way which went through the dark woods at the end of the cemetery I knew he was up to something. I got the mail and started back for the house. Came back down the drive-way through the woods and past the cemetery. Nothing happened. As I got closer and closer to the house I thought maybe he wasn't going to do anything after all because he would've done it in the spookiest section of the drive-way. When I was almost to the house and walking past our car and relaxed now that nothing had happened my uncle jumped out from in front of our car and hollered "BOO!" Scared me so bad I almost peed myself. I didn't think I was ever going to quit screaming or that he was ever going to stop laughing.

BOOM!!: Back in the 1960s, the boyfriend that I had before Gene, had a cherry bomb that he wanted to set off. He had had it for years buying it when they were still legal. Some time after he purchased it they became illegal. So we hatched up a mischievous plan. He brought it over to the house one night and he and I sneaked through the fence into the cemetery that was right by my parents yard. We found a large tombstone to hide behind. Since the cherry bomb was old we didn't know if it would even explode. It did! He lit it and gave it a toss and it made an earth shaking BOOM!! The neighbors across the street yanked their front door open to see what happened but he and I were hiding behind that large tombstone trying to keep from giggling too loud. The neighbors finally slammed their door shut but no one in the neighborhood ever said anything about it.

CEMETERY SERMON: One summer day we heard someone talking in the cemetery but just thought it was a person visiting a loved one's grave. But after awhile the voice became louder and louder so we went out to the yard to see what was going on. There was a man pacing back and forth, holding his open bible in one hand and waving his other upraised hand in the air. It looked like he was preaching a fire and brimstone sermon – to dead people.

* * * * * * * * * * * * * * * * * * *

VOODOO: In the spring of 1995 we took a trip to New Orleans. While there we took a voodoo tour. We also visited a voodoo temple and met a real voodoo priestess. She and her pet python were very nice - didn't hex anybody or anything. But, just to be on the safe side, everyone in the tour group, including us, made a monetary donation to the voodoo god of their choice!

We also toured the cemetery where the famous, historic Voodoo queen, Marie Laveau, had once been entombed. Some years ago a tradition was started and is supposed to bring good luck. One breaks a brick from a nearby tomb and uses it to mark an "X" on Marie Laveau's tomb. Her descendants however were extremely unhappy with this practice. I wanted to mark an x on the tomb but also wanted to respect the family's wishes so I just marked an imaginary x on it with my finger. Gene video taped it and I didn't realize till we got home and I watched the video that I approached the tomb in a very apprehensive and fearful manner. When our trip came to an end and it was time to head for home we considered staying another few days in New Orleans but then decided to go ahead and leave. And just in time too. It was cloudy the day we left and soon after the area was hit with heavy rain and disastrous flooding that made national TV. Maybe marking that "X" the way I did really brought us luck after all!

THE LEGEND OF THE WHITE WITCH: Back when we had some money (many years ago) we took a cruise to Jamaica. Our tour included a visit to Rose Hall. If you ever get to Jamaica it is a must see. It is a large beautiful mansion built in the 1700s. As the legend goes it was the home of the white witch Annie Patterson who came there in 1820. Annie became the wife of John Palmer the owner of Rose Hall.

Annie was a young beautiful Irish woman who was taught voodoo and witchcraft as a child by her nursemaid who was a Haitian priestess. John Palmer was the first of three husbands murdered by Annie by either poisoning, stabbing or strangling. She also tortured and killed numerous slave lovers when she became bored with them.

Annie was strangled in her bed during a slave uprising in 1831. It is said that she still haunts the house to this day. Some people say it is all fictitious while others say it is partly true. In the basement of the mansion we were each served a glass of witches brew. I took a sip and thought the top of my head was going to blow off so I didn't drink anymore or I would still be laying there drunk.

We then were taken on a tour of the first and second floors. I did not know prior to the tour that Rose Hall was once owned by a Henderson. I don't know if they are connected to my Henderson line or not.

While visiting the tomb of the supposed witch a lady in our tour group who had sampled a bit too much witch's brew climbed up and laid on top of the tomb to see if she could conjure up any spirits. Much to her disappointment (and the relief of everyone else) nothing happened.

GO TO HELL: After visiting Rose Hall in Jamaica we went to Hell. Yes, you read it right It was a hell of a nice place and we had one Hell of time! Now I can truthfully say "I've been to Hell and back." And if anyone ever gets mad enough at me to tell me to "Go to Hell!" I can reply with, "Been There, Done That!"

MISCELLANEOUS

HAUNTED LOG CABIN IN CRAWFORD COUNTY: In 1837 the two year old granddaughter of Washington County resident Abraham Brinker was murdered by a slave in Crawford County. The story that I was told was that the slave, Mary, had heard that her master John Brinker was going to sell her. So in retaliation while Mr. and Mrs. Brinker were away Mary drowned their little girl in the spring. I was told the little girl, Vienna, was buried directly behind the cabin as her mother wanted her close. However some say she was buried or was moved to the family cemetery.

Mary was caught trying to drown another Brinker child but the father was able to stop her before the child died. A record of Mary's trial is at the courthouse in Steelville. She was eventually hanged for her crimes. It is said that the cabin of John Brinker is haunted.

BIGFOOT SIGHTED IN IRON COUNTY: This is from an **1881** newspaper: A strange story comes from the west end of the county. A young man named Strickland attended by his dogs, started out hunting Friday morning of last week. Mr. S. lives in Dent Township, about twenty miles west of Ironton. A short distance from home his attention was arrested by an object lying in the leaves on the ground, but he was about to pass by thinking it some domestic animal, when it rose to its feet facing him. The object had the face of a human being and was entirely without clothing. Its body was covered with long dark hair, which streamed in the cool wind, like the mane of a horse. As soon as it rose, the strange being started off at a run, Mr. Strickland calling out after it. His first thought was to shoot it, but hesitated until it got out of range. The dogs then took its track, but Mr. S. called them back, and went home pending over his strange encounter. It was proposed to get up a hunting party and scour the woods thoroughly in search of the stranger, but up to date no additional developments have been made. Mr. S. is a truthful man, and asserts his willingness to make affidavit of the matter herein contained.

OUT-OF-BODY-EXPERIENCE: The day that my father died (11 September 1976) I had an out-of-body experience. My mother and I were at St. John's hospital out in the garden area getting some fresh air. We had been at the hospital for about 6 days. I laid down on a park bench in the nice warm September sunshine and dozed slightly. The next thing I knew I was floating maybe 30 - 50 feet or so above myself. I could look down and see myself lying on the park bench. I wasn't afraid as it all felt so peaceful. Then I heard my mother's voice telling me we better go back inside. I opened my eyes and was back in my body again. We went into the hospital and when we walked past the nurse's station on the way to my father's room the nurse stopped us. She said that they had been trying to locate us and had been calling our home phone and looking around the hospital to let us know that my father was dying. I forgot about the out-of-body experience for sometime thinking it must have been a weird dream until one day I read an article in a magazine about out-of-body experiences. I immediately thought of my experience and thought OMG! That article totally described what I had! Until then I had never even heard of out-of-body experiences.

ANOTHER OUT- OF- BODY EXPERIENCE: With this experience I had been in bed for days very sick with the flu. I had a bad cough and the doctor had prescribed cough syrup with codeine in it. This was the first time I'd ever taken codeine. When that medicine kicked in the next thing I knew I was floating above the bed just inches from the ceiling. I took my finger tips and reached up thinking, "Ohhhhh, I can touch the ceiling!" But before I could actually touch it I was back in bed again feeling very drowsy and went to sleep.

TIC TOC: When I was a teenager I could not wear a wrist watch. Any time I put a watch on my wrist it would stop ticking. When I took it off and laid it on the table it would start working again. I developed the habit of carrying the watch in the pocket of my bluejeans. One time after getting back from a long horseback ride I tossed my bluejeans along with some other clothes into the washing machine. Later I put them in the dryer. It wasn't until I went to iron them that I discovered my watch or pieces of it my pocket. That commercial that says that a Timex watch, "Takes a licking and keeps on ticking" isn't exactly accurate.

BUSY GHOST: Anonymous states that they knew someone who lived in a haunted house. Every time they would leave the house to go shopping or out for the evening they would come home and find that the ghost had re-arranged all of their furniture. Now if they could just get it to wash dishes and do laundry.........

SOURCES: An Overland Journey To The West - Jacquelyn Smith, National Register of Historic Places, Washington County Spanish Grants, Judy Moyers & staff at Washington County Recorder of Deeds, The History of Bellevue Valley, Wikipedia, Ozarks Watch, The Daily Journal, Obituary of Augustus Jones & a Sketch Of His Life from the Iowa Daily Telegraph, Chicago Historical Society, Ancestry.com, The Argus – Winona County Historical Society, MyHeritage.com, Ozark Mountains, History & Culture – Ozark National Scenic Riverways, Missouri – DNR, Potosi Abstract, The St. Francois Mountains - Missouri's Hard Rock Core, Missouri Historic Towns, Census, Goodspeed's History of Washington County, Missouri, Missouri Ghosts, The Miners Prospect, Topozone, Native American Tribes of Missouri, Native American History, Missouri History, The Weekly Independent, Mysteries of the Unexplained, Iron County Register, Place Names Of Five Southeast Counties Of Missouri, Washington County Place Names,

1928-1945, St. Louis Post Dispatch, Coroner's Inquests for St. Francois County, Picture of Lemp Mansion by Paul Sableman, Wikipedia Commons, History of Kimmswick, El Camino Real, St. Louis: A Fond Look Back,

Hallie Ramsey, Lindell Akers, Almeta "Pepper" Buis, Pamela Allen, Pat O'Hanlon Ramsey, Cindy Merx, Sue Breakfield, Anne DeShane & Josh McRaven, Leslie Hamby, Pat Brown, Terry Nixon, Blanche Owens, Lisa Rulo Mitchell, Tammy Rulo Davis, Donnie Heth, Judy Myers, Gary Foree, Malinda James, Anonymous x 3, Personal experiences of Esther Ziock Carroll

ABOUT THE AUTHOR

I have been doing genealogy/history research since 1971 and have compiled quite an extensive and interesting family history with trails leading to the countries of Canada, France, England, Ireland, Scotland, Germany, Italy, India, Egypt, Labrador, Mosquito Coast of Nicaragua and the Caribbean Islands of St. John, St. Thomas and St. Croix.

My ancestors include medieval knights, soldiers from the French and Indian War, the Revolutionary War, the War of 1812, the Civil War, WWI and WWII. Also clan chiefs, a Lord, Barons, a Baroness, a sheriff, a marshal, weavers, farmers, plantation owners, merchants, preachers, Moravian Missionaries, moonshiners, a gangster and ancestral associations with such well known historical figures as George Washington, President John Adams, Daniel Boone, Davy Crockett, Joseph Smith and Brigham Young, Gens. Wm. T. Sherman and Ulysses S. Grant, Gen. Sterling Price, Sam Hildebrand, William Clarke

Quantrill and Jesse James.

I have written extensively about my genealogy, also about the history of Washington County. My articles have been published in local newspapers and numerous history books.

I am a former genealogy instructor at Mineral Area College and have a Certificate of Tennessee Ancestry, a Certificate of Illinois Ancestry and a certificate of Washington County, Missouri ancestry. I have assisted other authors by providing historical information for their writing projects which were later published.

I have been on numerous paranormal investigations with various groups. I had a brief appearance in the paranormal documentary The Unknown Resident by Dark Level Productions. Even though I am not mentioned in the credits I also assisted with historical research for the documentary The Haunted Boy, a film by Spooked Productions.

In addition to my research and writing projects

I am also a servant to 13 spoiled rotten cats (all stray rescues) Licorice, Miss Kitty, Calico, Matt, Dillon, Smokey, Momma Kitty, Voodoo, Hoodoo, Tom & Jerry, Banshee & Ittybittykitty, one old lazy dog, and one very tolerant husband.

I have written numerous articles but my most well known articles include:

Washington County, Missouri In The Civil War

The Most Outrageous Crime Ever
Committed In Washington County

The New Madrid Earthquakes
Of Southeast Missouri

Carnage At The Crossroads
The Tragic Story Of Sgt. Cecil J. Cash

ADDITIONAL PICTURES

Haunted Pond – John Smith Road

Mysterious Stones On My Property

Rear View of Bust Mansion

Long Family Plot

James Long

Big River Bridge At Blackwell

Old Building At Blackwell

Railroad Tracks At Blackwell

Road signs of what are supposedly very
haunted roads.

Entrance to Meramec Caverns

Gene Carroll at Gads Hill

Made in the USA
Columbia, SC
27 June 2017